Charles Dickens Nason

Schools of the Society for the Propagation of Christian Knowledge

among the Germans of Pennsylvania. Vol. 1

Charles Dickens Nason

Schools of the Society for the Propagation of Christian Knowledge
among the Germans of Pennsylvania. Vol. 1

ISBN/EAN: 9783337256944

Printed in Europe, USA, Canada, Australia, Japan

Cover: Foto ©Paul-Georg Meister /pixelio.de

More available books at **www.hansebooks.com**

The Schools

of the

Society for the Propagation of Christian Knowledge
Among the Germans of Pennsylvania.

TABLE OF CONTENTS.

Introduction,

The Immigrations,

The German Church-Schools of Colonial Pennsylvania,

The Rise of the Society for the Propagation of Christian
    Knowledge among the Germans of Pennsylvania,

The Schools Established,

The Decadence and Closing of the Schools,

Conclusion,

Bibliography,

Chapter I.

INTRODUCTION

THIS paper is to deal with the Schools of the Society for the Propagation of Christian Knowledge Among the Germans of Pennsylvania. The schools were in active operation from 1755 until about 1760 and one, at least, until 1763. The complexity of the educational conditions in colonial Pennsylvania as well as the meagre details of the movement that are generally known challenges discussion. The materials are not readily accessible but the interest in local history has preserved a few fragments which facilitate the study. Recently the work of the historians of the Reformed Church has aroused considerable interest in the subject but, although biographers and historians frequently mention the work of the Society, as yet there has not appeared a treatment of the schools from the point of view of the educator.

The writer desires to acknowledge the assistance he has received from many friends, new and old. To Mr. Frank Reid Diffenderffer of Lancaster, to Dr. James I. Good and Prof. William J. Hinke both of Ursinus Theological Seminary, Philadelphia, and to Dr. Joseph H. Dubbs of Franklin and Marshall College is due the credit of bringing to light most of the new sources he has been permitted to use; to Professor Albert F. Smyth of the Cen-

tral High School, Philadelphia, who has acted as an inspiration to him in his higher education, he wishes to express his gratitude; and, especially, to Professor Martin G. Brumbaugh, of the University of Pennsylvania, who has been his Mentor, he owes his heartfelt thanks for many suggestions and for his continued encouragement.

Pennsylvania enjoys the distinction of possessing the best delineation of her educational history of any State in the Union. True, in Massachusetts, much has been written concerning individual movements in education and the name of Horace Mann, the great American reformer, is a nucleus around which has gathered a good sized library, but a complete history of education in Massachusetts is yet to be written. (Cf., Martin: Evolution of the Massachusetts Public School System, Preface). Not so, however, in Pennsylvania. In Wickersham's History of Education in Pennsylvania, we have the educational history of the Keystone State carefully and, for the most part, adequately and dispassionately presented. Valuable as it is, the book has one fault which will always condemn it in the eyes of future enquirers: Throughout there are scarcely any references to the sources from which the facts are drawn. Then too, a vast amount of information which has only lately become accessible was, of course, unknown to Superintendent Wickersham and the size of his volume did not permit a minute discussion of relatively unimportant topics. It is for these reasons, and for these reasons only, that I venture to rewrite a small part

of the history of education in Pennsylvania. Although the schools of which I am to treat were short-lived, they have an importance altogether incommensurate with the scant ten pages which Wickersham accords them.

If for no other, a good reason why the schools of the Society for the Propagation of Christian Knowledge among the Germans of Pennsylvania should be treated is that in the details of the scheme we have a dim foreshadowing of the system of public schools which was not finally inaugurated until nearly a century afterwards. Pennsylvania was slow in adopting a system of public schools and the chief blame for her tardiness is always laid at door of her German population and, perhaps, rightly so. And yet, it may still be a question in the minds of some if popular education, as we now understand it, is necessarily the best possible institution for the purposes in view. While we are laughing at the Philistines, we ought not to be unwilling to ask why they have such strange notions and even, if necessary, to go the weary road of tracing the course of the early development of our present system of public instruction. The reasons for their antipathy are sure to come to light. Fortunately a study of the conditions under which the schools we are to consider were founded, reveals the causes for their lack of sympathy for the public school system. But to present so small a gain at so great a cost would be unjustifiable were it not that, incidentally, there will arise from the study a clearer comprehension of the difficulties presented to ed-

ucators in colonial Pennsylvania and, I hope, an estimate of the German population more just than has usually been formed.

Whatever prejudices the writer may have introduced into this discussion, it certainly cannot be maintained that _Germanomania_ is one of them. So far as he is aware, he has not had a German ancestor since the days of Hengest and Horsa. This note seems necessary since a great deal of the present-day discussion of the Germans in colonial Pennsylvania is vitiated in that the writers are usually of German descent and are almost always in an offensively defensive attitude.

In order to treat the subject as briefly as possible, it will be necessary carefully to avoid entanglement either in the political wrangling from which the schools sprang or in the religious discussions which flooded the colony with pamphlet and counter-pamphlet, sermon and counter-sermon until one's head swims in the contemplation of the possibilities of religious argument. The history of the schools is the political history and the church history of the period between 1750 and 1763, but these will be mentioned only in so far as an understanding of the situation renders necessary.

This limitation is the more difficult because colonial Pennsylvania presents a most interesting example of the formation of a Commonwealth from many diverse elements. Besides the English, we have the Germans, the Swedes, the Welsh, and the Scotch-Irish as

prominent factors. The Germans, in their conservatism, desired to live by themselves in clans, whereas the Swedes, Welsh, and Scotch-Irish mingled with the English and, although they were absorbed by them, they participated in their advances. Holding aloof from general affairs, and uninterested in the activities of English town-life, the Germans lost many incentives to improvement and, accordingly, remained on the dead-level of mediocrity. They devoted their whole energy to the conquering of the forest, the tilling of the soil, and the advancement of their material prosperity. The result has been that they have left their impress on two of the richest agricultural counties of the United States and the presence of their red barns is a sufficient guarantee of the productivity of the soil surrounding them. Yet in the midst of plenty, they forgot their posterity. The greatest fault of the colonial Germans was that, in withdrawing from the life of the outside world, they doomed their descendants to plod on in the same weary furrows in which their own lives were spent. So completely was their development stopped that in the districts now settled by the Pennsylvania Germans, there survive many of the customs of the Reformation and in Pennsylvania, to-day, there is represented more of the old Germany of two hundred years ago than in the Fatherland itself. (Cf., Pennypacker: Historical and Biographical Sketches; Fisher: Making of Pennsylvania, pp. 117-125).

Conservatism was not confined to the Germans. The Friends, too, have been greatly blamed for their passive attitude. The

community of religious interests between the Friends and most of the German sects gave them a political advantage which they were slow to see out which, once recognised, they never forgot. In time of preparation for war, the Non-resistents found themselves well able to maintain their stand so long as they held stubbornly together. The exasperation of the practical politician before this invincible body of religionists can be better imagined than described. They were English and Scotch-Irish and accordingly must have had a genius for governing and for fighting; can you blame them for some show of anger when they saw their genius thwarted at every turn? It is chiefly through the notes of rage they sounded in their broadsides, the printing of which kept Franklin's presses hot, that the present-day reader of history has learned to call the German pioneers, "barbarians", "ignorant boors", "savages", and other similarly impolite epithets. The feeling on both sides ran high. The years immediately preceding the French and Indian War furnished too severe a test for the principles of non-resistence and the Friends, with the Germans, retired from the government, leaving the bloody business of war to those for whom the work was more congenial.

With the close of the war, the schools of the Society for the Propagation of Christian Knowledge among the Germans of Pennsylvania also closed. The connection between the two events will become clear as we advance. What became of the Society and its funds after the closing of the schools is not apparent. The most

current supposition is that the money was turned over to the German Department of the University of Pennsylvania which was reorganised in 1779 but of this I can find no proof. It has been supposed, too, that Franklin College, now merged in Franklin and Marshall College, grew out of a classical school established by the Society at Lancaster; but, as Prof. Joseph H. Dubbs remarks, there is a very inconvenient interval of silence separating the two institutions. (Dubbs: Old Franklin College, p. 165). It is quite probable that neither institution owes very much directly to the system of charity schools but a study of them may throw considerable light on the beginnings of elementary and higher education in Pennsylvania.

Having indicated a few of the difficulties we shall encounter as we go on, we now proceed to our more immediate purposes. First we will briefly review the conditions of the immigrations, following this with a sketch of the Church education among the German colonists. With these to serve as a background, we will then sketch in so much of detail as our knowledge and the size of the canvas permit. The drawing must remain incomplete and blank places will frequently appear but its general meaning will be sufficiently apparent.

Chapter II.

THE IMMIGRATIONS

IN DISCUSSING the history of education among the Germans of colonial Pennsylvania, there are two general considerations which must be borne well in mind. The first is the peculiar constitution of the colony and the second its heterogeneous population. Growing out of the religious freedom guaranteed by William Penn combined with the movements of Dissent in the churches of Europe, and the impoverished condition of Germany after the Thirty Years' War, there came to Pennsylvania's shores an immigration differing greatly from that of the colonies to the north or to the south. Like the sturdy New Englanders, many of the early immigrants came in search of religious liberty and many in the quest of homes for themselves and their families but, later, the cupidity of land speculators and transportation companies entirely changed the character of the population. The principal activity of these colonisers was directed toward the bringing over of Germans and it is with these Germans that we have exclusively to deal.

In his two journeys on the Continent, Penn became well acquainted with the peculiar religious views of many sects among the Germans and found them to a great extent in agreement with the fundamental principles of Quakerism. When the territory of Pennsyl-

vania fell into his hands, he naturally turned to his friends in
Germany with an offer of an asylum where they might worship without interference from the State. The Palatinate had suffered terribly during the Thirty Years' War. It is estimated that before
the war the population was half a million but at its close there
were less than one-tenth that number. (Sachse: The Fatherland,
p. 95). Since the treaty of Westphalia, October 24, 1648, only
three confessions were tolerated; the Catholic, the Reformed, and
the Lutheran. Other denominations were denied all privileges and
little time was wasted in measures of conciliation. Fines, imprisonment, banishment, and death followed quickly upon the discovery of secret meetings; and yet, in spite of the persecutions,
this period of fifty years had been one of great religious fomentation so that a catalogue illustrating the various shades of religious belief would be long indeed. (Spener in his "Freyheit der
Gläubigen," Franckfurth-an-Mayn, 1691, enumerates the following
sects of Separatists: Weigelians, Rosicrucians, Arminians, different kinds of Syncretists, Osianderians, those who would not
take religious vows; Pseudo-Philosophers, Anti-Scripturalists,
Latitudinarians, Chiliasts, and Boehmists. (Sachse: The Fatherland, p. 142).' The sects which were thus formed were driven to
meet secretly in order to avoid persecution and, in return, their
secrecy was assigned as the cause of their danger to the State.
When they learned that William Penn was to tolerate all religions
in his colony, the magnitude of the emigration was limited only by

its expense. Penn carefully looked after the welfare of his German settlers and even when, in the middle of the eighteenth century, the foreign population threatened to absorb the English, the Proprietaries advised great concideration in the criticism of the Germans by pamphlets or otherwise. In the summer of 1709 Penn announces to his Secretary, Logan, the coming of a body of Germans and advises him to use them "with tenderness and care" as they are "a sober people, divers Mennonites, and will neither swear nor fight."

In these immigrations a large number of educated men came over but we must not permit the presence of a few men like Pastorius, Kelpius, and a half-dozen others to blind us to the fact that the bulk of the immigrants were men of low mental and moral standards. There were two fairly distinct periods of immigration. In the beginning, say from 1682 to about 1738 we have small numbers of Pietists, Moravians, Mennonites, Tunkers., Schwenkfelders who were in every way desirable settlers, some of them men of good education and all living lives of moral simplicity; but at the close of this period there begins another which may be said to extend to the outbreak of the Revolution. From 1756 to 1761 there were no immigrations owing to the danger of a sea voyage during the war between France and England. In Rupp's Thirty Thousand Names there are no entries for these years. In this second period large numbers of Germans were brought over as Redemptioners, i.e., immigrants who were sold for a term of years to the highest bidder to

pay their passage. It was not because they were poor and hence Redemptioners that often they became undesirable colonists but because they were of a class of people likely to be overreached by the grasping business methods of the transportation companies which employed agents, known as Neulanders, who picked up the colonists promiscuously in German cities and brought them to America often under false pretenses. After they were once on board ship it became only too evident that they were carried as a speculation and not for the benefit of the colony where they were to land. Much as we may pity the plight of these poor deluded creatures, we cannot ascribe to them great mental powers as a palliative for their injuries. A glance through the pages of Rupp's Thirty Thousand Names will reveal the number of names written by the clerk and not unfrequently half the passengers were unable to write.

Most of the early emigrants made their way from the Palatinate first into Holland where frequently they sojourned for a considerable time before going on to England which was regarded as an intermediate resting place on their journey to America. In 1709, fully 10,000 were encamped near London and the next year over a thousand of these settled on the Hudson at Schoharie. They were greatly aided in London by the Rev. Anton William Boehme who was court preacher in the royal chapel, St. James. In the later emigrations under the care of the transportation companies, the journey was made without this intermediate stop. These emigrations on a large scale reached their height about 1750. In the summer and

fall of the preceding year, nineteen thousand Germans arrived. "So long as I was there (1750-1754)," writes Gottlieb Mittelberger, "from 20 to 24 ships with passengers arrived at Philadelphia alone every autumn, which amounted in four years to more than 25,000 souls, exclusive of those who died at sea or since they left home."

(Reise nach Pensylvanien, Eben's trans., p. 37). Almost every ship load carried one or more preachers and schoolmasters since the transportation agents found it much easier to entice the Germans over if at the head of their list they had the name of a minister. When it was at all difficult to get a minister or a schoolmaster to come, the embarrassment was overcome by hiring some adventurer to play the part. These men formed a special class of scamp preachers and schoolmasters who tramped around from place to place teaching, or preaching, or practicing medicine as long as the caprice or the ignorance of their patrons allowed. It was this class of men that gave the regular ministry so much trouble. The Rev. Henry Melchior Mühlenberg who had charge of the Lutheran churches in Pennsylvania says, "It teems with a wicked, frivolous rabble and vagabond preachers and students, and the devil is raging and carrying on his slanders and calumnies against the poor Hellenses."

Beside the direct immigration from Germany, a great many colonists came in from Georgia and New York. Those coming from Georgia were almost exclusively Moravians although a few Lutherans, the Salzbergers, made their way to Pennsylvania; The special priv-

ileges which had been granted in Georgia to the Moravians caused so much trouble with their more warlike neighbors that, in 1738, some of them paid back the money that had been advanced them and came to Pennsylvania; these were followed two years later, by the rest of the Georgia Moravians settling at Bethlehem and at Nazareth. From New York came a large number of the Germans who had been settled on the Hudson at Schoharie in Queen Anne's time. They had become exasperated at the intrigues of the New York governors and chose Pennsylvania because of the greater freedom that was promised. These people were chiefly the Lutherans and Reformed that settled at Tulpehocken in 1723. (cf. Cobb: The Story of the Palatines).

After the settlement of Germantown, the German immigration spread into Montgomery county settling Skippack, Falkner's Swamp (New Hanover), Trappe (New Providence), and Goshenhoppen. Lancaster and Oley in Berks county were settled about 1710. The Schwenkfelders came in 1734 locating principally in what is now Montgomery, Berks, Bucks, and Lehigh counties. The German settlements spread so rapidly over the colony that what are now Chester and Delaware counties were the only districts comparatively free from them.

that of friars. . . It was certainly a very right policy to encourage the importation of foreigners into Pennsylvania, as well as into our other colonies. But it has been frequently observed, and, as should seem, very justly complained of, that they are left still foreigners, and likely to continue so for many generations. And they have schools taught, and books printed, and even the common newspaper in their own language: by which means as they possess large tracts of the country without any intermixture of English, there is no appearance of their blending and becoming one people with us. This is certainly a great irregularity, and the greater, as these foreigners, by their industry, frugality, and a hard way of living, in which they greatly exceed our people, have in a manner thrust them out in several places; so as to threaten the colony with the danger of being wholly foreign in language, manners, and, perhaps, even inclinations. In the year 1750 were imported into Pennsylvania and its dependencies 4,317 Germans, whereas of British and Irish but 1,000 arrived; a considerable number if it was not so vastly overbalanced by that of the foreigners.

"I do by no means think that this sort of transplantations ought to be discouraged; I only observe, along with others, that the manner of their settlement ought to be regulated, and means sought to have them naturalized in reality." (Burke: Account of European Settlements in America, Works, ix, p. 345, Boston Edition).

In a letter to Archbishop Secker, November 27, 1759, the Rev. William Smith, Provost of the College of Philadelphia, from the resources at his command makes an estimate of the membership of each denomination. He seems to find it necessary to account for the religion of each individual, there being no division left for non-church-members, viz:

1. Of the Church of England about	25,000
2. Quakers	50,000
3. English, Scotch and Irish Presbyterians, Covenanters, &c	55,000
4. English Anabaptists	5,000
5. German Anabaptists, or Menonists, and other Quietist Sects	30,000
6. German Lutherans, who are well inclined to be incorporated into the Church of England	35,000
7. Swedish Lutherans, who use the Liturgy & discipline of the Church in most Articles	5,000
8. German Presbyterians or Calvinists, who style themselves the Reformed	30,000
9. Roman Catholics, English, Irish and German	10,000
10. Moravians, and a small German Society called Donkers, about	5,000
In all	250,000

(Smith: Life of William Smith, i, p. 220).

The relative importance of the various denominations in Philadelphia is shown by the enumeration of churches in 1749:

1 Episcopalian

2 Friends

1 Swedish

1 Dutch Calvinist

1 Roman Catholic

2 Presbyterian

1 Baptist

1 Dutch Lutheran

1 Moravian

(Watson: Annals, ii, p. 404).

We read in our histories that the liberal spirit of the founder of Pennsylvania called to his colony all denominations and creeds, and that consequently the Pennsylvania colony was composed of the oppressed of all countries. Most prominent among the foreign element were the Germans. We have seen how ship-load after ship-load came over until, April 23, 1747, Governor George Thomas in a letter to the Bishop of Exeter estimated that three-fifths of the population were natives of Germany. (Rush: Manners of the German Inhabitants, p. 5). As most of these were adherents of sects having a close affiliation with the Friends, in time of war-preparation, the German vote was usually against the Proprietary side, or "governor's men." This strong peace party in the colony exasperated the more pugnacious opposition so that they bent every energy towards undermining the Quaker influence, and in assimilating the foreign element. In this endeavor it was undoubtedly Benjamin Franklin who exerted the most potent influence. He has given us a

picture of the antagonism between the English and the Germans. Writing March 20, 1751, he says, "Already the English begin to quit particular neighborhoods surrounded by the Dutch being made uneasy by the disagreeableness of dissonant manners; and, in time, numbers will probably quit the province for the same reason. Besides, the Dutch under-live and are thereby enabled to under-work and under-sell the English, who are thereby extremely incommoded, and consequently disgusted, so that there can be no cordial affection or unity between the two nations." (Franklin's Works, Bigelow, ii, p. 221).

And again, in his letter to Peter Collinson, May 9, 1753:--"I am perfectly of your mind that measures of great temper are necessary with the Germans, and am not without apprehensions, that, through their indiscretion, or ours, or both, great disorders may one day arise among us. Those who come hither are generally the most stupid of their own nation, and as ignorance is often attended with great credulity, when knavery would mislead it, and with suspicion when honesty would set it right; and , few of the English understand the German language and so cannot address them either from the press or pulpit, it is almost impossible to remove any prejudices they may entertain. Their clergy have very little influence on the people, who seem to take pleasure in abusing and discharging the minister on every trivial occasion. Not being used to liberty, they know not how to make modest use of it, . . . They are under no restraint from ecclesiastical government; they

behave, however, submissively enough at present to the civil government, which I wish they may continue to do, for I remember when they modestly declined intermeddling with our elections; but now they come down in droves and carry all before them, except in one or two counties.

"Few of their children in the country know English. They import many books from Germany, and, of the six printing-houses in the province, two are entirely German, two half German half English, and but two are entirely English. They have one German newspaper, and one half German. Advertisements intended to be general, are now printed in Dutch, (German) and English. The signs in our streets (Philada.) have inscriptions in both languages, and some places only in German. They begin, of late, to make all their bonds and other legal instruments in their own language, which (though I think it ought not to be), are allowed good in our courts, where the German business so increases, that there is continued need of interpreters, and I suppose in a few years, they will also be necessary in the Assembly, to tell one half of our legislators, what the other half says.

"In short, unless the stream of importation could be turned from this to other colonies, as you very judiciously propose, they will soon so outnumber us, that all the advantages we have, will, in my opinion, be not able to preserve our language, and even our government will become precarious." (Franklin's Works, Bigelow, ii, pp. 296-295).

The danger was a real danger. Unless Pennsylvania was to become a German colony, some radical measures must be adopted. One that suggested itself was the restriction of the suffrage to such Germans as should be able to speak English, but so great a storm of opposition arose that it was impracticable to push the matter farther. If such direct measures could not be made use of, then recourse must be had to some deeply laid scheme. This was the scheme of the charity schools. Franklin was the man best fitted to undertake such a plan and although his name is not frequently mentioned in the records that have come down to us, there are striking similarities in language in this letter I have just quoted and the report of William Smith who acted as the Secretary of the Philadelphia Trustees of the Society for the Propagation of Christian Knowledge Among the Germans of Pennsylvania. Certain it is that Franklin was a large factor in the scheme, if he was not the power behind the throne.

Chapter III.

THE GERMAN CHURCH-SCHOOLS OF COLONIAL PENNSYLVANIA

THE religious life of the German colonists presents many points of interest and for an understanding of their position on educational questions some statement of the connection of their religion and their schools is necessary. Beside the church, and inseparably connected with it, there was always the school and the character of the school depended upon the character of the church. But the religious conditions in the colony were very complex.

The religious unrest of the seventeenth century in Germany gave rise to that form of Christianity which has been denominated Pietism. In every church there are individuals having a tendency to belittle denominational differences and to magnify the importance of religious feeling and good works. These tendencies found their first serious expression in the beginning of the seventeenth century in the writings of the Lutheran divines, John Arnd and John Andrae, and in the words of the Calvinist, Cocceius; but Philip Jacob Spener and Augustus Herman Francke were the chief exponents of that form of Pietism which made its way to America. In the history of the movement there have been many cases where its prophets were of doubtful sanity and in general it may be said that too great importance was attached to the feelings and mere opinion of its votaries. Moreover, it led to a distrust of the regular

ministry and fostered a spirit of carping criticism in such of the hearers as were of insufficient mental capacity to realize the full meaning of their faith. Its fundamental tenet that "Christianity is first of all Life" was opposed to the dogmatism of an established clergy but when combined with a sturdy common-sense, it became a mighty instrument for good. It is not to be understood, however, that Pietism was itself a sect of the Lutherans. It had its adherents among other denominations, and the Jansenism of Holland, (Reynier Jansen, one of Pennsylvania's first printers, was of the same family as Cornelius Jansen, Bishop of Ypres, the founder of the sect bearing his name). the Quietism of France, and the Quakerism of England, were results from much the same causes as the Pietism of the Lutheran denominations. (Sachse: The Fatherland, p. 115. See Bigelow: Molinos the Quietist)).

It was particularly among the educated classes that Pietism gained adherents and when persecution followed, many of these came to America. February 13, 1694 (O. S.), ten years after the founding of Germantown, a party of forty mystics under the leadership of Magister Johannes Kelpius, arrived in Philadelphia. Almost the whole company were students who had been driven from the German universities because of their heretical opinions, and tradition says that their peculiar dress--the students' gown--aroused considerable curiosity. They settled on some land given them on the banks of the Wissahickon, and formed a celibate community which was known to the outside world as the Society of the Woman in the

Wilderness. These hermits of the Wissahickon desired to live apart that they might prepare themselves for the coming of the heavenly bridegroom. They built a tabernacle on one of the bluffs overlooking the stream. It contained a large room, or saal, for religious meetings and a schoolroom. There were also stalls for the use of those who wished to retire for meditation. Surmounting the whole structure was a Sternwarte, or observatory, in which there was always someone watching for the secondcoming of Christ.
(Sachse: German Pietists in America, p. 71).

We know very little of the active teaching work done by the members of the Society of the Woman in the Wilderness, but the mere presence of such persons of so great acquirements could not but have an effect upon their neighbors. Kelpius, himself a young man of less than thirty years, was master of four languages besides his theological lore, and the other members of whom we know anything were men of no mean ability. The inventory of the estate of John Seelig who was Magister after Kelpius mentions " 5 Bibles, 14 books, 10 works of Jacob Boehme, 120 Latin, Dutch and Greek Books." The character of the man is shown in a letter to Francke, August 7, 1694: "What pleases me here most is that one can be peasant, scholar, priest, and nobleman all at the same time without interference, which of all modes of living has been found to be the best since patriarchal times. To be a peasant and nothing else is a sort of cattle-life; to be a scholar and nothing else, as in Europe, is a morbid and self-indulgent existence; to be a

priest and nothing else makes godless and riotous." And further: "For we are resolved, besides giving public instruction to the little children of this country, to take many of them to ourselves and have them day and night with us, so as to lay in them the foundation of stable, permanent character. With them the beginning must be made, otherwise there will be only mending and patching of the old people." (Pa. Mag. Hist. and Biog., xi, p. 439; see Sachse: The Fatherland, p. 159, note).

In a rather incoherent letter to Stephen Momfort, a Baptist clergyman with whom Kelpius corresponded, he writes: "The children under the Information and Tuition of Pietists (for the Students applied themselves chiefly to the Education of children, as they do to this day with great, yea extraordinary success) begun to reproof their Parents if they was working and Lye or unrighteousness! yea some in their tender years came to witness strange things of the Invisible worlds---" From such statements as these and from the stray references that we have of the different individual members of the community, we are led to conclude that the Society devoted considerable attention to teaching. Although their religious views were not of a character to make them acceptable teachers to many, yet they were frequently employed as private tutors in the neighboring families. Their method of teaching morals was peculiar. Kelpius had printed a set of cards each of which bore a moral sentiment and whenever an oath or an evil action was committed in the presence of a member of the brotherhood, the pack,

known as a Schatzkästlein, was presented, and the guilty person was required to draw a card. It was believed that Chance would select the proper sentiment. As the cards were always placed upon the tongue there arose the saying that "the Pietists ate their religion." Sachse: German Pietists in America, pp. 100-102). They were but a small band of enthusiasts, and with the great influx of Germans, this educational movement inaugurated by Kelpius was unable to cope.

Somewhat resembling the Kelpians, especially in their mystic tendencies, was the Society of the Seventh Day Baptists. Early in the eighteenth century, a body of men and women under Conrad Beissel settled in Lancaster county at a place to which they gave the name, "Ephrata". Here they established a monastic religious order. The purposes of the society were not primarily educational but as several of their number were persons of considerable learning, there became attached to the monastery, in 1733, a classical school in which were taught also music and German. Many children from Pennsylvania and Maryland and even from abroad were sent to this school. Besides this secular boarding-school they had also a Sabbath-school started by Ludwig Höcker, in 1740, full forty years before Robert Raikes, in England, gained the renown of having established the first Sunday-school. This Sabbath-school at Ephrata continued its sessions down to September, 1777 when the building

(This building was named, "Succoth"). which it occupied was given over to hospital uses.

Conrad Beissel, whose cloister name was Father Friedsam Gottrecht, was somewhat of a musician and he introduced into the monastery a peculiar music which was written in several parts--sometimes as many as seven. This music was a mighty instrument in their religious services and its peculiar moaning, resembling the sounds of an Aeolian harp, attracted many curious listeners. The sisters in the convent wrote out the music in books which furnish excellent examples of the survival in America of the mediaeval art of illuminative writing. In their note-books they wrote many hymns of their own composition all after the style and imagery of the Song of Solomon which served as a model for their mystic effusions.

But it is as a printery that Ephrata is particularly interesting in the history of education in Pennsylvania. Although the issues of the Ephrata press commenced in 1745 with a mystic work by Beissel, it is probable that they had a press at an earlier date. Most of the books were dissertations on theological topics or hymn-books. In 1748 was issued van Braght's "Der Blutige Schau-Platz", the largest book of colonial times. The work was translated from the Dutch for the Pennsylvania Mennonites by (John) Peter Miller, the prior of the monastery, (There exists a tradition
 that Peter Miller was employed by the colonies to translate
 their Declaration of Independence into the court languages of
 Europe.) and fifteen men were employed for three years in the

printing and binding of the volumes. The Ephrata press continued in active operation down to the outbreak of the Revolution. (Cf. Seidensticker: Ephrata eine Klostergeschichte; also, First Century of German Printing in America. Pennypacker: Historical and Biographical Sketches. Chronicon Ephratense).

Many schools were carried on by the Moravians and education in their hands attained an advanced stage. The typical Moravian school was a small boarding-school the teachers of which devoted their lives to their work, very much according to the fashion of the Jesuits. The "room-teacher" lived with his pupils and had entire charge of them when they were not under the different masters. Many such schools were founded, and, as early as 1748, there were fifteen of these schools. The modern survival of this method of education is seen in the Moravian schools at Bethlehem and Lititz where the aim is not at all to adapt the pupil to the requirements of fashionable society but rather to develop a sturdy common-sense and a practical piety. They very much resemble the Friends in their educational ideal, yet, true to their German traditions, they give a large place to music. These schools gained a great reputation, scholars coming to them even from the West Indies, and, frequently, the number of applicants for admission exceeded the capacity of the schools.

It was not only in secondary education that the Moravians were active, but they had neighborhood schools wherever there were settlements to patronize them. Spangenberg is himself said to have

established thirty of these little schools, and in his enumeration of the population of Bethlehem, in 1756, he mentions sixty-two persons employed in the schools as attendants or as tutors. The curriculum was limited to the three R's, study of the Scriptures, and music, but, on the other hand, the teachers were not mere hirelings; they were men and women who regarded teaching as a part of the missionary work of their church. In the education of the Indians, too, they were very active and it is chiefly through the educational work of the Moravian missionaries that we known anything concerning the dialects of some of the Indian tribes. The Moravians are a splendid example of missionary zeal well directed.

There were other smaller denominations that did considerable educational work. Thus the Schwenkfelders, the Mennonites, the Tunkers, and others supported schools but they were all church schools and the Societies were too small to make much of an impress on the heterogeneous population. The Tunkers, however, were large contributors to the Germantown Academy and a Tunker bishop, Christopher Sower, Jr. (The spelling of this name appears first as Saur, then Sauer, and finally in the English form, Sower, which is the spelling now employed by the descendants.) wrote on educational topics and published many books. The most famous teacher in early Pennsylvania was Francis Daniel Pastorius, a Mennonite. Not only was he a very learned man, a master of seven or eight languages and well read in law, science, and philosophy, but he was also a successful teacher working for seventeen years among

the Friends in Philadelphia and in his own school in Germantown. The first schoolbook written in Pennsylvania, no copy of which is to be found, was written by Pastorius and published in 1700. Another famous teacher was Christopher Dock, also a Mennonite. To him we owe the first Pennsylvania work on pedagogy, "Die Schul-Ordnung," published by Christopher Sower, Jr., in 1739.

The Lutherans and Reformed have the reputation of being the most progressive denominations among the Germans of colonial Pennsylvania. Although their cause suffered a great deal from the vagabond preachers who came over in the immigrant ships, yet, as soon as the mission churches of America were organized, the education of the children became a matter of serious concern to the ministers. Beside every church there was a school-house and these parochial schools were probably as good as the corresponding schools in Germany. In the outlying congregations, the school-master came before the minister, adding to his duties as teacher, that of reading a sermon before the congregation on Sunday. Indeed, most of the native ministers served an apprenticeship in teaching a parochial school. The schools were in every sense mission schools. Usually there were from twenty to forty children, although at some places as many as sixty were in attendance, and the session extended through the winter months.

Among the Lutherans the influence of the Halle Orphanage, that magnificent collection of charitable institutions founded by Augustus Hermann Francke, was most potent. A great many of the ear-

ly ministers and teachers had been trained in the Halle Pädagogium and they brought to Pennsylvania the methods and ideals of the great Pietist. Naturally enough the chief aim of their schools was a practical one, a training to meet the immediate needs of their pupils, yet the cultivation of the religious nature was never lost sight of and the schools were regarded as the great bulwark of the church. Not only did Halle help Pennsylvania by sending over teachers, but frequently there came money and books to aid the schools in the wilderness. Among the Reformed, the greatest influence in establishing parochial schools was the missionary zeal of the Rev. Michael Schlatter. He visited all the congregations placing ministers and establishing schools. Unlike most of the other German denominations, the Lutherans and Reformed required an educated ministry, because, in order to uphold their doctrinal differences, an accurate knowledge of the Scriptures was necessary. Indeed, all the early ministers had received their theological training in the universities of Germany and many of them were men of commanding talents who left their native land to labor as missionaries among their countrymen in Pennsylvania. (Thus

Mühlenberg is said to have spoken Latin, Swedish, Dutch, German, French, and English and to have been familiar with Greek and Hebrew.) The great care with which they were selected by the authorities in Halle secured a body of especially able men.

The chief activity of these denominations was in the work of the elementary schools; they had no academies such as that of the

Seventh Day Baptists at Ephrata, or of the Moravians at Lititz, Nazareth, and Bethlehem, but in many cases the minister taught higher branches to those who desired to enter the ministry. The details of such private instruction are not to be had, although many statements in the lives of the early ministers refer to this mode of training. The hardship of having to send their ministers to Germany for their education, caused the Lutherans in 1773 to found a theological school which continued in operation for but three years. There were thirteen scholars in the first year and the curriculum was quite comprehensive, including, besides English and German, Latin, Greek, Hebrew, History, Mathematics, and Elocution. The schools of the Lutherans and Reformed were so well organized that, although the Society for the Propagation of Christian Knowledge among the Germans of Pennsylvania was undenominational, it was upon their foundation that they sought to build.

The school buildings and equipment in colonial times were at best meagre, and especially is this true of elementary schools. A log structure sometimes with two or three rooms for the accommodation of the teacher and his family, surrounded by the teacher's garden was considered an ample provision for the housing of the scholars. The Lutheran school at Trappe (New Providence) is representative. Says Mühlenberg, "The neighbors and renters, armed with broad axes, hand mauls and wedges, assembled to build the school-house. Some felled trees, others notched the logs and put them in place, and still others split clapboards, or shingles, for

the roof. Some sought out and hauled shapely stones for the fireplace, and others prepared sticks and mud for the chimney. The building was about eighteen by twenty-two feet, one story, seven feet high, built of rough logs, with the cracks daubed with mortar, called "kat and clay". The floor was made of split logs, roughly hewn, called puncheons; the hearth was of stone, about four feet wide and as long as the width of the fire-place, the back wall and sides of the fire-place being also of stone. At the hearth a piece of gro... was left without a floor to afford the scholars a place to stick their goose quills to make them of uniform pliability. There was one ledge door in the side of the building, with wooden hinges and latch. The windows ran the whole length of the side or end of the building, three to twelve inches high, with little posts set in a foot apart, on which oiled paper was pasted in lieu of glass. Slanting writing boards were fastened along the walls, even with the under edge of the windows, and the scholars mounted slab seats, without backs. A short, slanting board in one corner near the end of the hearth constituted the school-master's desk. During the noon hour the boys split up the logs for kindling wood."

There were no blackboards although chalk, in large lumps, not in crayons, was used to mark the music score upon the walls, and Christopher rewarded his pupils by marking upon their hands with chalk as a certificate of their good behaviour, which was to be seen at home and to receive a suitable reward. There were no

steel pens. Every writer in the school had to go up to the master to have his quill cut for him, no one else possessing a pen-knife. There were no blotters, but fine sand was sprinkled over the copy. The text-books used were usually the New Testament, the Psalter and the Catechism.

With these crude appliances, the routine of the school was naturally primitive and yet, from the very simplicity of the conditions, the schools derived an element of strength. With comparitively few pupils, but ranging from four to twenty years of age and at all stages of development, the work was necessarily individual. A few minutes' attention to each, leaving the rest of the time for study, was doubtless a tax on the master, not only because he was required to be ubiquitous in his attentions, but also because the leisure of his pupils gave ample time for the mischief Severe punishment was the rule, flogging for the worst offences and for minor misdemeanors the culprit was placed before the class ornamented with leather spectacles, with horns and peices of fur pasted over the eye-brows. These were the Booksbrille which was the German substitute for the dunce-cap. There was also in a corner an immense fur cap like a drum major's chapeau, under which the delinquent was required to stand, the punishment consisting in that lice were supposed to drop down on the youngster's head. These are but the mere externalities of the life of the schools but they are practically all that has come down to us.

For the regulation of the teachers, certain rules were adopt-

ed which are interesting since they take us into the colonial school-house, where the teacher "must be qualified in reading, writing, arithmetic, and singing---he must undergo an examination in these branches and be approved. He must be one that takes a lively interest in, and helps to build up the Christian church; and must be also a God-fearing, virtuous man and lead an exemplary life. He must teach six hours per day---three in the forenoon, and three in the afternoon---unless the number of scholars increases, when he must give them more time. He must be judicious and adapt himself to the various dispositions, and gifts of the children; and exercise patience, love, and gentleness, as much as possible in his teaching, that he may win their hearts, and work with blessing among them. He shall at all times open and close his school with a hearty prayer to God for his grace and blessing. Besides teaching the children to read and write, he shall also train them to pray, and exhort them to continue the practice. Besides the above-mentioned school rules, the school-master obligates himself, in the absence of the minister, or in the case of his sickness or inability to preach, that he will read some verses of Scripture, &c., to the edification of the congregation. He shall also be the chorister and organist, and during the services all is committed unto him". These rules reflect the primitive conditions of the schools and at the same time a purity of purpose and a high ideal of the teacher's function in the community which would be a credit to any age.

In return for all these services, he is to receive 28 p. year from the church and five shillings per quarter for tuition from the pupils, although the Elders reserve the privilege of sending children whose parents cannot afford to pay, for three shillings per quarter out of the church treasury. (From the rules of the Reformed Church in Philadelphia, drawn up in 1760 by the Rev. Mr. Steiner. See Van Horne: Reformed Church of Philadelphia pp. 80-85). At Trappe the school-master had several perquisites: "He shall occupy the school-house in quiet possession and have free firewood. He shall have the right to cultivate and use as much of the three acres of the church and school land as may be indicated and permitted by the vestry. He shall receive the collections taken up on the two high festivals of the year, viz., Easter and Whitsunday, for organ-playing. At church weddings he shall take up the collection with the "klingelsack" and have the same for playing the organ. He shall enter the names of baptised children in the church record regularly and neatly, for which he shall receive a "gratial" from those who are not poor and are willing and able to pay". (Kretschmann: Old Trappe Church; Chapter on the Parochial School.)

Almost everything we have said in this chapter confirms the statement that the church and the school were intimately connected. A school separated from church control is a recent novelty in educational administration; the old schools before the Reformation were all church schools although in the middle of the fifteenth

century references to secular schools occur. After the Reformation the old custom could not be broken. In the church community it was necessary to secure some education in order that a knowledge of the Scriptures might not perish, and the different denominations naturally wanted to control the teaching of their children. Thus there grew up the system in which the teacher was simply the assistant of the minister, serving as the leader in the singing, the organist, and the janitor of the church and school buildings. The system had many advantages, especially in that the minister of the congregation became the supervisor of the schools, and to the minister and the vestry, all complaints against the master were to be directed. As many of the teachers were serving an apprenticeship for the ministry, they carried on their work as teacher and student under the same master. Of course anything like uniformity was out of the question and, in colonial times, at least, the introduction of a system for use in all the schools of the colony would have been not only impolitic but unwise.

When we remember the necessarily hard life of the settler in a new country, the work in education done by the denominations becomes of considerable importance. They can scarcely be called an ignorant, boorish people---if they were, why were so many German books printed in Pennsylvania and why were so many others imported? They gained their evil reputation because their language was not understood by their critics, to whom also their religious princi-

ples seemed fanatic. They undoubtedly lacked the zeal of the Scotch-Irish and they were not as well educated as the Friends, but our review of their educational institutions shows that they are not to be regarded as dwelling in intellectual darkness. After this inventory of some of the more significant examples of educational activities among the colonial Germans, we are now ready for a consideration of the comprehensive scheme of the Society for the Propagation of Christian Knowledge among the Germans of Pennsylvania.

Chapter IV.

THE RISE

of the

SOCIETY FOR THE PROPAGATION OF CHRISTIAN KNOWLEDGE AMONG THE GERMANS OF PENNSYLVANIA

WE HAVE now to discuss the attempt which was made by the English to force upon the Germans their language and, incidently, their customs. As soon as the desirability of the union of the heterogeneous elements of the Pennslyvania colony became evident, the reformers, as is natural, first turned to the schools. Thus there arose a system of German-English schools. This interference in the school affairs of the Germans did much to lessen their activity in educational matters since it relieved them of the responsibility of maintaining the old church schools by offering to them for the time a system of charity instruction. When the wave of reform had passed, matters fell back into a state worse than before the German-English schools were started.

As necessary for an understanding of this scheme, we will sketch first the general moral conditions among the Pennsylvania Germans.

The Church, more especially the Moravians and the Lutherans, early became interested in the religious welfare of the Pennsylvania colonists, and sent ministers over to inquire into their spir-

itual condition. As early as 1734 the Moravians sent over George
Boehnisch, a missionary, to the Pennsylvania field; he was followed in 1735 by Spangenberg, who became well qualified to speak of
the conditions of Pennsylvania. (He visited in Pennsylvania and
Georgia, 1735 to 1739; resided in Bethlehem and Philadelphia,
1744 to 1749; came again to Pennsylvania and North Carolina from
1751 to 1759, and once more resided at Bethlehem, 1754 to 1762.)
These men gave such gloomy reports, that the Moravians organized a
Society in London, May 8, 1741, to provide funds for prosecuting
the work among the Germans. The Board consisted of James Hutton,
Rev. George Stonehouse, John Ockershausen, John Bray, and Augustus
G. Spangenberg, with Adolph von Marshall, Secretary, and William
Holland, Servitor. This Society continued to hold monthly meetings until 1751, when it was dissolved. The Society, however, was
reorganized in 1768, and continues to exist. This Society has
always been purely missionary. (Smith: Life of William Smith, i,
pp. 43, 44. See also Benham: Memoirs of James Hutton, p. 70.)

Somewhat later, Nov. 25, 1742, the Lutherans sent Henry Melchior Mühlenberg to look after their colonial churches. Mühlenberg received his theological training at Göttingen and in
Francke's Orphanage at Halle. He was a man of tremendous energy,
and spent his life in carefully organizing the churches and schools
of the Lutherans. His "Reports" made to the Fathers at Halle are
anything but encouraging. Speaking of New Hanover in 1742, he

writes in his diary: "Since ignorance among the youth is great in this country, and good school-masters are very rarely found, I had to take this matter also into my hands. Those who might possibly teach the children to read are lazy and given to drink, use all sorts of books to make their sermons, waste their time, preach, and administer the Lord's Supper merely to get cash in hand. It is a shocking sin and shame. I requested the congregation to send me first the older children, as I intended to go about among the three congregations, remaining in each successively one week. On the following day, Monday, Jan. 10, the parents brought me some of their children. It does not look very promising to see youths of seventeen, eighteen, nineteen, twenty years of age appear with the A-B-C book. Yet I rejoice in seeing the desire to learn something. Singing also has totally died out among the young people." (Mann: Life of Mühlenberg, p. 130.)

Gottlieb Mittelberger, a Lutheran school-master who was teacher and organist at New Providence and Philadelphia from 1750 to 1754, thus writes: "The most exemplary preachers are often reviled, insulted and scoffed at like the Jews, by the young and old, especially in the country. I would, therefore, rather perform the meanest herdsman"s duties in Germany than be a preacher in Pennsylvania. Such unheard-of rudeness and wickedness spring from the excessive liberties of the land, and from the blind zeal of the many sects. To many a one's soul and body, liberty in Pennsylvania is more hurtful than useful. There is a saying in that coun-

try that 'Pennsylvania is the heaven of the farmers, the paradise of the mechanics, and the hell of the officials and preachers.'"

(Mittelberger: Reise nach Pensylvanien. Translation by Eben, p. 63).

The Rev. Michael Schlatter of the German Reformed Church arrived at Philadelphia, September 6, 1746. He held toward the Reformed Church much the same relationship that Mühlenberg held toward the Lutherans. He was a young man from St. Gall, Switzerland where, seven years before, he had been licensed as a preacher. Since then he had been acting as tutor and assistant pastor in various places; among others in Amsterdam. When the Classis of Amsterdam decided to take the organization of the Pennsylvania churches into their own hands, they chose Schlatter for the important service of visiting all the German congregations, organizing their churches, placing ministers over them, opening parochial schools, and forming a Coetus (or Synod). In his celebrated "Appeal" in behalf of the Reformed in Pennsylvania, he states that he travelled over eight thousand miles on horseback in the performance of his duties. (Harbaugh: Life of Michael Schlatter, pp. 84-234 for the text of the "Appeal"). Schlatter reported that he found very few churches, and that parents were unable to educate their children. Since the number of pupils in such schools as did exist was so small, the master had to support himself by working at some other calling, thus banishing to the teacher's desk only such persons as were dismal failures in other walks of life. Al-

though many wished to have their children educated, the distance of the schools made it impracticable for them to send their children, and in many places the parents were becoming indifferent to education and in danger of becoming semi-barbaric. (Harbaugh's Life of Schlatter, p. 77, 178).

Schlatter reported these facts to the Fathers in Holland, and in his visit to Europe in 1751 and 1752, he awakened such an interest among the Reformed that the Synod of North Holland presented an account of the destitution to the Government, requesting that a general collection might be taken up in the Netherlands. The Synod of South Holland as well as the Classis of Amsterdam were also active. To aid the collection, Schlatter's "Appeal" was printed in Dutch and German, and later, translated into English by the Rev. David Thomson, one of the English ministers in Amsterdam. The Reformed Church in Holland, as a result of Schlatter's representations, received from the States General in

1751, 2,000 florins for five years.
1756, 2,000 florins for three years,
1759, 1,600 florins for two years,
1761, 1,000 florins for two years, a total of 21,400 florins. The Synods of North and South Holland started a fund amounting (1781) to 14,000 florins and the Classis of Amsterdam commenced a fund which, in 1755, was 17,795 florins. Besides the subsidy from the States General, the Reformed Churches in America received the interest on these synodical and classical funds having an aggre-

gate principal of nearly $13,000. (Hinke: The Parochial School at
Reading, in the "Reformed Church Record", February 22, 1908).

These funds it must be confessed were exclusively for the benefit of the Reformed Church. A very frequent source of confusion has been the supposition, entertained more especially by the early historians of the Lutheran and Reformed Churches, that the money which was afterwards collected in England and Scotland was turned over to the Holland Synods and from thence made its way to America. This is not the case. These funds (there were at least four of them) were kept carefully distinct and the money collected in Holland continued to go the the support of the Reformed congregations through the media of the Classis of Amsterdam and the Synods of North and South Holland, whereas the money collected in England was used as an undenominational charity, although the sympathies of the administrators were largely Episcopalian. Thus there were a number of different religious bodies all having as one of their purposes, the intellectual and moral welfare of the Pennsylvania Germans.

It was only as a result of the agitation among the Reformed that the people of England learned of the destitution among the German settlers in Pennsylvania and chiefly it was through the preaching of the Rev. David Thomson. Mr. Thomson was a Scotchman who had charge of the English church in Amsterdam and he was deeply moved by Schlatter's report to the Classis. Accordingly, in the spring of 1752, he started on a journey through England and

Scotland in order to stir up an interest in the Pennsylvania churches. He was very successful, receiving permission to take up a national collection in Scotland which yielded twelve thousand pounds sterling. From the King, George II., he received a contribution of a thousand pounds; from the Princess of Wales, a hundred pounds; and the Proprietaries pledged fifty pounds per annum. For a year Mr. Thomson was actively gathering money for the schools. Moreover, the collection continued on the Continent, the Reformed in the Palatinate giving three hundred guilders, the Swiss and al. contributed, and small sums came from individuals. The fund increased so rapidly that Mühlenberg, writing in 1754, states the aggregate at that time to be twenty thousand pounds. This is undoubtedly an exaggeration and arose because Mühlenberg supposed the Society was using only the interest on the fund whereas the probability is that they were spending their money nearly as fast as it came in.

The English church in Amsterdam became impatient at the long absence of their pastor in England and, finally, peremptorily called him back to his charge. Mr. Thomson on his return to Holland, desired to leave the money he had collected in the hands of some manager in London who would continue the collection and supervise its disbursement. Several prominent men in England, who had contributed largely, also undertook to manage the charity. These were the original members of the Society for the Propagation of Christian Knowledge among the Germans of Pennsylvania and the

new Society was an outgrowth from the Society for the Propagation of the Gospel which had been in existence for half a century. The men composing the new Society were the Right Honorable Earl of Shaftesbury, the Earl of Morton, the Earl of Finlater, and Lord Willoughby of Parham; Sir Luke Schaub, and Sir Joshua Van Neck, Baronets; Mr. Commissioner Vernon, Mr. Chitty, and Mr. Fludyer, Aldermen of London; John Bance, Robert Ferguson, and Nathaniel Paice, Esquires, of London; the Rev. Benjamin Avory, LL.D.; the Rev. Thomas Birch, D.D., the Rev. David Thomson, and the Rev. Samuel Chandler who was elected Secretary of the Society. (Pennsylvania Gazette, February 25, 1755).

These gentlemen were doubtless actuated by the purest of motives and, at this first stage in the development of the Society, there is not the slightest suggestion of any ulterior aims in the establishment of the schools. The reported condition of the Germans was so bad that ordinary humanity demanded that these settlers in America should be helped. It will be remembered, too, that England, in Queen Anne's time, sent over a great many Germans as a national enterprise and, accordingly, she felt some direct responsibility. Then again, it was to the advantage of England to keep her own people at home and at the same time to settle her colonies, therefore the influx of the Germans was a double gain. The least she could do would be to make the conditions in the colonies pleasant for both her English and her foreign colonists. Surely they could never work together for common ends until all

understood the same language; and it was this phase of the movement which gave to the schools their linguistic aims. They were
to be German-English schools, the understanding always being, however, that the German was finally to speak English, not the Englishman to speak German.

Some of the Germans also saw the advisability of their countrymen becoming acquainted with English as a matter of simple business policy. In and around Philadelphia this motive was strong,
as the markets, where English was a necessity, were held two days
in a week, but in the outlying districts there was no such incen-
tive since all business was transacted in German. Then, too, the
presence of churches and schools in which their own language was
used, and of books and newspapers printed in German prevented them
from seeing that they were to a large extent cut off from the interests of their neighbors of other nationalities, and the few
voices raised in favor of a knowledge of English were scarcely
heard. Pastorius sought to render the learning of English easier
for his children by giving them a large manuscript volume written
in Greek, Latin, German, French, Dutch, English, and Italian. Urg-
ing upon his children the necessity of learning English, he thus
addresses them: "Though you are (Germano Sanguine nati) of High
Dutch parents, yet remember that your father was naturalized, and
ye born in an English Colony, consequently each of you <u>Anglus na-
tus</u>, an Englishman by birth. Therefore, it would be a shame for
you if you should be ignorant of the English tongue, the tongue of

your countrymen."

Since, among the congregations, the influence of the minister was great, it was particularly the German preaching which prevented the spread of the English language, an influence which is still powerful in the German sections of the Commonwealth. Accordingly, the Society in London announced it as their first purpose to aid Protestant ministers, particularly among the Lutherans and the Calvinists. These men were to receive rewards especially if they preached one sermon a week in the English language, although their stipend was to be largely conditioned upon the poverty of their congregations. This aspect of the charity afterwards fell into abeyance and the schools alone received aid. In the "Memorial in the Case of the German Emigrants" published in London, 1754, which, not being intended for the German readers, differs in many particulars from the "Brief History of the Rise and Progress of the Charitable Society" published in Philadelphia, the objects of the schools were stated as follows:--

1. That the schools shall be equally for the benefit of the Protestant youths of all denominations, without exception.

2. That they shall be instructed in the English and German languages, in writing, and keeping common accounts, in singing of psalms, and the principles of the true Protestant religion, and in those catechisms, which are respectively approved of and taught by the parents and ministers of the denominations they belong to.

3. That the inspection of every school shall be committed to a

certain number of reputable persons, living near the places where such schools shall be fixed, to visit monthly or quarterly each particular school and to send an account of the state and progress of them to the Trustees General in Philadelphia to be transmitted from them to the Society here.

5. That they, the said Trustees, shall make a general visitation of all the schools, once every year at which one or more of them have resolved to be present.

6. That the Rev. M. Michael Schlatter, in whose capacity and zeal for the service the Society have the best reasons to be satisfied, shall be appointed to act under the direction of and accounting to the said Trustees, as Visitor and Supervisor of all the said Schools, as he is a German by birth, understands both the English and the German languages, is acquainted with the state and temper of the German emigrants, hath already taken incredible pains in preaching to and instructing them, hath formed them into several distinct congregations, is well known and respected by all the several denominations of them, as having lived amongst them and been highly serviceable to them for several years past in Pennsylvania, and is thereby peculiarly capable of suggesting what measures from time to time may be serviceable to be taken, to bring them into proper regulation and order.

7. The said Trustees have also represented it to the Society here as their opinion that it might be of great service to religion and industry to have a few schools also for girls and to

encourage some schoolmistresses to teach the reading and use
of the needle. (Cf., Harbaugh: Life of Schlatter, pp. 272-277;
Smith: A Brief History of the Rise and Progress of the Charitable Scheme and A Memorial in the Case of the German Emigrants).

In order to keep down denominational animosities, it was decided that the two chief denominations, the Lutherans and the Reformed, should agree upon their school-house and, if possible, choose a master to their liking before receiving aid from the Society. For the first year, schools for boys at Reading, York, Easton, New Providence, Skippack and Hanover, with an equal number of Girls' schools, were projected. The masters of the boys' schools were to be allowed a sum not exceeding $20 per annum and the mistresses were to be paid $12. Not more than $500 was to be allowed for the year's expenses, and after the salaries of the masters and of the superintendents were paid, whatever was left was to be apportioned among the ministers according to their deserts, "the Society intending to make no other difference in the distribution of their charity but what the wants and merits of those who shall be thought the proper objects of it shall render advisable and necessary." The Reformed seem to have been the only ministers who received aid from the fund, the only help the Lutheran ministers received being, in a few cases, a small salary as catechists to the schools. The minutes of the Coetus of the Reformed Church in Pennsylvania for the year 1756 acknowledge the receipt of $91 for their ministers, $80 was the sum given in 1757 which was re-

peated in 1758 and 1759. After this date the contributions to the ministers ceased and the opposition of the Reformed to the movement began.

Another project of the Society was the sending over of Bibles, spelling-books, and the catechisms of the different denominations for use in the schools. Afterwards they sought to supply the demand for books of this character by the establishment of a press in the colony but, although this part of the project was carried out, the issues of the press of the Society did not include much of value.

The schools in Pennsylvania were to be merely elementary schools but it was recognised that it might be advisable to give some of the pupils a higher training which could be done least expensively in the Philadelphia Academy but provision was also made for the education of five or six of the best pupils in the University of Oxford although no one seems to have taken advantage of the privilege.

It is at this point that the Rev. William Smith appears upon the scene. William Smith was a young Scotchman who came to this country in 1751. The year before he published a "Memorial for the Establishment of Parochial Schoolmasters in Scotland, addressed to the great men in Parliament, etc." He was a man of considerable education, a graduate of Aberdeen University, and came to this country as the tutor of the two children of a New York gentleman. When he had been in New York a little over a year and had just passed his twenty-sixth birthday, he published a little pamphlet

on education which attracted the attention of Richard Peters and
Benjamin Franklin. It was entitled "A General Idea of the College
of Mirania", its purpose being to map out a curriculum for King's
College, now Columbia, which was then projected. Franklin was
struck with the ability of the young man and soon secured him as
teacher of Natural Philosophy and Logic and, later, after he had
taken Orders, William Smith took entire charge of the Academy and
Charity School which afterwards became the University of Pennsylvania.
His election to the faculty took place May 25, 1753 and in
December of that year he was in London. His stay in Pennsylvania
was not more than four months. This fact is necessary as throwing
light on a letter which is to follow in which Smith shows considerable
acquaintance with the conditions in Pennsylvania. In all
probability the seeming acquaintance with the German population of
Pennsylvania was gotten at second hand and we cannot but suppose
that his information comes in general from his correspondent,
Benjamin Franklin.

Mr. Smith went to England to be ordained and was in London before
any definite plan of action on administering the charity had
been decided upon. It was mainly through his instrumentality that
the money went directly to the organization of German-English
schools. As he was a recent arrival from Pennsylvania, his opinions
were accorded considerable weight and his position in the
Church of England and his former connection with the Society for
the Propagation of the Gospel made it possible for him to gain a

hearing in influential quarters. This was especially fortunate because the new Academy and Charity School of Philadelphia was not at that time in a flourishing condition and Smith wanted to do what he could toward helping it. This could best be done by furthering the project of the charity schools since it was at the Academy of Philadelphia that the teachers for the schools were to be educated. Accordingly we find him putting forth every effort to hasten the cause of the schools and, because of his visit, the Established Church took a deeper interest in the educational movement. Whether this was because Smith urged the possibility of bringing the Lutherans into the Episcopal Church seems uncertain. Most potent in interesting the Church of England was a letter which, December 13, 1752, the Rev. William Smith addressed to the Society for the Propagation of the Gospel in Foreign Parts. Some of the more significant passages I quote:

"My Lords and Gentlemen: For many years past incredible numbers of poor protestants have flock'd from divers parts of Germany & Switzerland to our Colonies, particularly to Pennsylvania. Their melancholy situation, thro' want of instructors & their utter inability to maintain them, with the distressing prospect of approaching darkness & idolatry among them, have been represented to their fellow protestants in Europe in the most moving terms.

"Indeed it is deeply affecting to hear that this vast branch of the protestant Church is in danger either of sinking into barbarian ignorance, or of being seduced at last from that religion

for which they and their fathers have suffered so much. And should ever this be their misfortune, their Liberty itself, with all their expected use to these nations, will be entirely lost. Besides this, their having no opportunity of acquiring our language, & their living in a separate body, without any probability of their incorporating with us, are most alarming considerations.

"In these circumstances, the Scheme you have entered in, to send instructors among this people, is of the greatest importance. The influence of a faithful clergy to form the social temper, to keep up a sense of religion, & guide such a people in their duty, is obvious. Nor is the institution of Schools for the education of their children a point of less, but perhaps still greater, importance.

"Without Education it is impossible to preserve a free government in any Country, or to preserve the Spirit of Commerce. Should these Emigrants degenerate into a state little better than that of wood-born savages, what use could they make of English privileges? Liberty is the most dangerous of all weapons, in the hands of those who know not the use & value of it. Those who are in most cases _free_ to speak & act as they please, had need to be well instructed how to speak and act; and it is well said by _Montesquieu_, that wherever there is most freedom there the whole power of Education is requisite to good Government. In a word, Commerce & Riches are the offspring of Industry & an unprecarious property; but these depend on Virtue & Liberty, which again depend on Knowl-

edge & Religion.

But further, Education, besides being necessary to support the Spirit of liberty & commerce, is the only means for incorporating these foreigners with ourselves, in the rising generation. The old can only be exhorted and warn'd. The young many be instructed and form'd. The old can neither acquire our language, nor quit their national manners. The young may do both. The old, whatever degree of worth they acquire, descend apace to the grave, & their influence is soon lost. The young, when well instructed, have their whole prime of life before them, & their influence is strong & lasting.

"By a common Education of English & German Youth at the same Schools, acquaintances & connections will be form'd, & deeply impress'd upon them in their cheerful & open moments. The English language & a conformity of manners will be acquired, & they may be taught to feel the meaning & exult in the enjoyment of liberty, a home & social endearments. And when once these sacred names are undestood & felt at the heart;--when once a few intermarriages are made between the chief families of the different nations in each county, which will will naturally follow from School-acquaintance, & the acquisition of a common language, no arts of our enemies will be able to divide them in their affection; and all the narrow distinctions of extraction, &c., will be forgot--forever forgot--- in higher interests."

Here follows a discussion of the power of education to form

the Nation by pruning off the useless and even hurtful characteristics of the people and by grafting in their place the useful and harmless qualities of mind. He takes as his illustration the heterogeneous Roman State which was unified and centralized into a commonwealth under the religious and social ceremonial introduced by the mythical Numa Pompilius.

"From what has been said, it appears that, in the present circumstances of the people under consideration, nothing but a common education of youth, can obviate the inconveniences justly dreaded. It is only this that can incorporate them, by teaching them a common language, giving rise to acquaintances & intermarriages, influencing their genius; & preserving, forming, or altering the principle of Government among them as public weal requires.

"The next things are the method of education, the government of the Schools, & the means of supplying & maintaining them in proper masters.

"The method of education is a point too important to be handled in the bounds of this letter, & shall be the subject of a separate essay. It is obvious that it must be calculated rather to make good subjects than what is called good scholars. The English language, together with writing, something of figures, & a short system of religious & civil truths & duties, in the Socratic or catechetic way, is all the education necessary to the people. These things therefore must be left open to everybody without price; but all other less necessary branches of literature my

have quarterly fees laid upon them, to prevent the vulgar from spending more time at school than is necessary. It is generally thought that the knowledge of <u>ethics</u>, civil & religious, is not to be acquired without languages, & laborious discussions, for which the bulk of mankind has neither the leisure nor capacity. But nothing can be a greater mistake than this; & it is to be feared that nothing has contributed more to the present general corruption of morals. Can it be possible that those great Truths & Duties, the knowledge & practice of which God intended as the means of making man happy & keeping Society together, are any other way above the vulgar reach, than as they have been made so by the imaginary distinctions & perplexing reasonings of men themselves? No. These truths & duties are founded on the most simple principles, the most obvious relations, & from thence may be deduced at no great expense of Time or Genius, without the aid of learned languages and laborious researches. The general principles of our common Christianity may, in a very short Compass be laid before youth, & the truths & duties thence resulting press'd more upon them as truly amiable for their own intrinsic beauty & happy tendency. The use & end of Society, the different forms of Government, the excellency of our own, with all the horrors of civil & religious tyranny, may be displayed to them; and from thence all social duties might be deduced, by a chain of the most clear & natural consequences. All this might be taught at leisure hours by a good master, during the 2 or 4 years the people otherwise

spend in learning to read, write, &c.; & it is hardly to be conceived how much such early impressions would contribute to make good men as well as good subjects. It is of little importance to Society how many recluses should know the theory of ethics, when they seldom launch into busy scenes of real life; but the virtues & practice of the vulgar is the strength of the State, so that without making these topics, above mentioned, a part of education, such schools will be wanting in the main point, the forming of good Subjects.

"2. With regard to the Government of the Schools, it is of the greatest use, in smaller Societies, where it is practicable, to have all places of Education uniformly govern'd by one sett of men, that so youth may be everywhere trained up in subordination to the public Sense. This trust can only be executed by men residing on the spot, & therefore 6 or 7 principal Gentlemen of Pennsylvania may be appointed Trustees-general for providing foreign protestants in that & other Colonies, with Ministers and Schoolmasters.

"One or more of these Trustees, is once every year to visit all the Schools & examine the Scholars, giving a small premium to one or more boys, born of German Parents, who shall best deliver an oration in English, or read an English Author, nearest to the right pronunciation. Let another premium be given to that boy, whether English or German, who shall best answer to some questions concerning religious & civil duties, on the plan already sketched out. . . .

"But further, as the success of all Schools depends on good discipline, & keeping up emulation, these Trustees-general should substitute six deputy-trustees for every school, 3 of them being English, & 3 Germans, for the sake of forming more connexions. These deputies should visit the Schools & bestow premia as above, one every month, transmitting an account of such visitations to the Trustees-general, & these last sending once or twice a-year an account of the whole state of the Schools to the Society in London. This scheme cannot fail of helping up discipline & emulation.

"2. The Masters for such Schools can only be found & educated in America. They must understand the English & high Dutch, with Mathematics, Geography, Drawing, History, Ethics, with the Constitutions & interests of the Colonies. Now, strangers cannot be thus qualified. For tho' they understand both languages, we could not be sure of their principles; nor would they for several years know the Genius of the people, or correspond with the general Scheme of Polity in the education of youth; nay, they might be sent from the <u>palatinate</u> or <u>Switzerland</u> to counterwork it, & defeat the desired Coalition. Clergymen, Schoolmasters, Physicians, &c., have a natural influence over the people in the Country, & the constant importation of strangers of these professions is impolitic. Such men should be educated under the Eye of the public in the colonies where they are wanted; & thus we will not only be certain of their principles, but also have them complete masters both of the English & German languages.

"It is a happy circumstance, in Pennsylvania in particular, that there is a flourishing Seminary, where such men may be educated; & happier still that the honble proprietary is to make a foundation for maintaining & educating constantly some promising Children of poor Germans as a supply of well-principled Schoolmasters, that must be acceptable among their friends.

"4. With regard to the maintenance of these instructors, that must come in a great measure from you. 'Tis true monies already collected in Holland, England, & Scotland will be no more than sufficient for a fair beginning; but you cannot fail of success in your application to the public Charity, to enable you to prosecute your Undertaking---an undertaking of far greater importance to the British--the Protestant interest--than can be well imagined at this distance.

"Figure to yourselves upwards of 100,000 strangers settled in our territory, chiefly by themselves, & multiplying fast;---strangers indeed to everything of ours; strangers to our Laws and manners; strangers to the sacred sound of liberty in the land where they were born, & uninstructed in the right use & value of it in the country where they now enjoy it; utterly ignorant & apt to be misled by our unceasing enemies & surrounded with such enemies to mislead them; &, what is worst of all, in danger of sinking deeper & deeper every day into these deplorable circumstances, as being almost entirely destitute of instructors, & unacquainted with our language, so that it is scarce possible to remove any prejudices

they once entertain. Nay, such prejudices may be daily increased
among them, unknown to us. They import many foreign books; and,
in Pennsylvania, have their Printing houses, their newspapers, and
of late their Bonds & other legal writings, in their own language.
In courts of Judicature, Interpreters are constantly wanted, thro'
the vast increase of German business, & may soon be wanted in the
Assembly itself, to tell one-half the Legislature what the other
half says. (Perry: Historical Collections, ii, 541-547).

Although the church schools were fairly good, there were not
enough of them and we have seen that there was a real need for
greater educational facilities in Pennsylvania, and yet we may
justly doubt if William Smith's scheme was well adapted to the advancement of education among the Germans. Schlatter, Muhlenberg,
and others report concerning the moral and religious destitution
of the colonists while Smith's chief argument in this letter and
in other places is that unless this body of Germans is Anglicized,
there is great danger that Pennsylvania will become a foreign colony, or that the Germans will turn Catholic and go over to the
French. It was even reported that one-fourth of the Germans were
Catholics and that Jesuit emissaries had been sent among them to
tempt the remainder to Catholicism by promises of the Ohio lands.
(Smith (?): Brief State of Pennsylvania, pp. 29-32, 37). To
William Smith this seemed a most telling argument and he frequently stated in his letters to the church authorities in England that
all the Germans cared for was a large farm, that they were so ig-

norant that they did not know any difference between the English
and the French government, and that even some of them had been
heard to say it made no difference to them which government was
over them so long as they were left in possession of their lands.
Moreover, he stated that the French had calculated on the apathetic character of the Germans and had settled Catholic Germans near
them in order to win their sympathies. In the event of the conquest
of the English, the French could ill afford to send over colonists
to settle their newly acquired lands and the Germans, being accustomed to the country and already settled, had still an added value
in that those who swore allegiance to France must adjure their allegiance to the British crown. From this point of view, once it
is granted that the education of the Germans would foster sympathy
for their English neighbors, the cause of the schools became the
cause of the British government and it was undoubtedly this extermist view which brought in contributions in such large amounts
from the British nobility. The attempt was even made by Smith to
bring the conditions in Pennsylvania before Parliament in the hope
that the schools might receive aid from the government, but it
seems never to have been pushed. (Smith to Archbishop Herring,

 Oct., 1754; Perry: Historical Collections, ii, 348-350).

  These reports reached the ears of the Germans and they were
not slow to resent the insult. On the succession of Robert Hunter
Morris as Lieutenant-Governor of the Province of Pennsylvania,
some thirty Germans, chiefly from the Lutheran and Reformed Chur-

ches, prepared an address in which they affirmed, in no uncertain words, their loyalty to the Crown of Great Britain. They claimed that no such accusation of disloyalty or conspiracy could be justly made against the Germans and challenged their accusers to place in evidence a single case of wrong-doing. And "now, hoping confidently that our Gracious King and Parliament are not moved in displeasure against us by any false insinuations, we entertain the good confidence to your Honor as a lover of justice and equity, to assist your humble servants in defacing such unjust clamours at home in England; and we hope our actions and loyal behaviour in this Province will always be sufficient proof of our tender affection to Great Britain." The sequel sustained the assertions of the Germans and proved the fears of the English to be groundless.

(Pa. Archives, 2d Series, ii, pp. 696-699).

At the time of the Colonial Wars there seems to have been a great desire to make the Protestantism of the Established Church of England synonymous with allegiance to the British Crown and this scheme for teaching the Germans "the knowledge of God" was calculated to further this desire. The whole movement was founded on the misapprehension that the Germans were liable to become Catholics. There was, however, a slight reason for this belief. The Moravians were closely associated with the Indians, very much as the Jesuits were; for this reason they were especially suspected. When the Indians afterwards committed atrocities, the feel-

ing against the Moravians increased. Then too, in the Oeconomy
of the Moravians the men and women had separate houses like con-
vents and their festivals of Easter and Christmas were so elabo-
rate as to make many believe that they were Romanists. The Moravians had to live under this suspicion until the breaking up of
the Oeconomy in 1762. (Trans. Mor. Hist. Soc., Series II, pts. 7
and 8, p. 337).

In a letter to the Governor of Pennsylvania, June 12, 1752,
Spangenberg sums up the charges against the Moravians under seven
heads and answers each in turn. The conclusion of the letter is
that the Moravians are Protestants seeking to convert the Indians.
While they very much dislike to interfere in governmental affairs,
because such action might prove prejudicial to their work of
preaching the Gospel, yet they were entirely devoted to the English
government. (Trans. Mor. Hist. Soc., Series II, pts. 7 and 8,
pp. 334-336). The Proprietaries did not share in these fears
that the Germans would overturn the government but they considered
it the part of wisdom to discountenance any criticism of the Germans unless under great provocation. (Thomas Penn to Richard
Peters, July 17, 1752; February 21, 17--: Penn Letter-Book).

There was another reason why Smith and his friends in the Episcopal Church wished to educate the Germans, especially "in the
constitutions and interests of the Colonies". Until recently, the
Germans, from their secluded position on their farms had taken little interest in affairs of state but the political turmoil was now

agitating even their bucolic breasts. At this time, the Proprietary Party, the Quakers, and the Germans, not to mention the Scotch-Irish, formed the centres of political disturbance. The Proprietary Party, composed chiefly of the Episcopalians, were in continual controversy with the Quaker government, and, with the approach of the French and Indian War, the struggle for supremacy became more severe. Since the peace principles of the Friends prevented their raising a militia for defense or voting money for war purposes, the Proprietary Party gained many adherents among people of plain common sense, the balance of power being maintained, however, through the gradually growing interest in politics of the peace-loving German sects who always voted with the Friends. But the moral question was not the only one involved, and the Germans "came down to the polls in shoals" to put the Quakers in office in part, at least, because a no-war policy meant no-tax-imposition. They were stirred up by their leaders to think that there was a design on foot to bring Pennsylvania under a militarism the evils of which they had experienced so long in the Fatherland; that the Proprietary Party had a design to enslave them, to take them away from their farms to work on the fortifications, etc., etc. Nowhere more clearly than in the gullibility of the Germans does it appear that a people with the same interests _must_ have the same language. The real questions at issue could not be intelligently discussed because neither side could make itself adequately understood by the other. But once the Germans had

learned their power, they became a factor to be reckoned with by the colonial politicians.

Certainly it was a statesmanlike policy to seek to make the people of Pennsylvania a homogeneous people and, although the Reformer always has at his command the school, even then the problem was not one easy of solution. It was too evident that the philanthropy of the administrators was that sort of charity in which the right hand is well aware what the left hand is doing and the almost malicious statements by which the claims of the schools were supported proves well enough that the zeal for the welfare of the Germans was not disinterested. The German-English school scheme was simply a cunning trap to catch the rising generation of Germans.

As a result of the representations of William Smith, the Society for the Propagation of Christian Knowledge among the Germans of Pennsylvania commenced active work. At this time the Society was composed of the Earl of Shaftesbury; Lord Willoughby, of Parham; Sir Luke Schaub, Bart.; Sir Josiah Van Neck, Bart.; Thomas Chitty and Thomas Fludyer, Aldermen of the City of London; Benjamin Amory, LL. D.; James Vernon, John Bance, Robert Fergusson, Nathaniel Paice, Rev. Dr. Biron, Rev. Caspar Weitstein, Rev. David Thomson, and the Rev. Samuel Chandler who was retained as Secretary. At the suggestion of Smith, several men representing the Proprietary Party in Pennsylvania, were appointed Trustees-General to take charge of the administration of the charity. These were James Hamilton, Esq., Lieutenant-Governor of Pennsylvania; William

Chapter V.

THE SCHOOLS ESTABLISHED

THE letter informing the Trustees, of .... just as Richard Peters and Benjamin Franklin were setting out to the treaty with the Five Nations at Albany, June, 1754, taking Conrad Weiser as interpreter. All work toward starting the schools accordingly was postponed until their return. August 10, 1754, the first meeting of the Trustees was held at the house of Mr. Allen at Mount Airy at which it was decided to establish schools at Reading, York, Easton, Lancaster, Hanover, and Skippack. For the local management of the schools six to ten deputies chosen from different denominations were to be selected at the next meeting, August 28, 1754. Those proposed were as follows:--

For Lancaster---Edward Shippen, Esq (English), President; Mr. Adam Simon Kuhn, Mr. Ctterbein, Mr. Sebastian Graff (Calvinist); Mr. Gera (Lutheran); Mr. James Wright, Mr. John Baer.

For New Providence and Skippack---Mr. Abram Sarler, Mr. John Diemer (Calvinist), John Schrack, Nicolaus Custer (Lutheran), Henry Pawling, Esq., Mr. Robert White, John Coplin (English).

For Reading---Mr. James Read, Protonotary, Francis Parvin, Esq (English Quaker), James Seely (English Presbyterian), Mr. Isaac Levan, Mr. Samuel High (Calvinist), Mr. Hans Martin Garick, Mr. Jacob Levan (Lutheran), Mr. Sebastian Zinwerner.

For Easton---Mr. Parsons, Mr. Lewis Gordon, Mr. John Chapman, Mr. John Le Fevre, Mr. Peter Trexler.

For New Hanover, Frederick Township---Andrew Kepner, Peter Krebs (Lutheran), Henry Antes, Esq., Mr. John Seifsnyder (Calvinist), John Potts, Esq., William Maugridge, Esq. (English).

For York no one was recommended but Mr. Weiser was instructed to communicate with interested persons.

For Vincent Township, Chester County---at the meeting, December 28, 1754, the following trustees were proposed, Sebastian Wagner (Calvinist), Michael Heilman (Lutheran), Conrad Snriter (Lutheran), Samuel Hover (English), Richard Richardson (English).

(Smith: Life of William Smith, J. II. 71, 72, 69).

No one took a deeper interest in the movement than Henry Melchior Mühlenberg who had already spent ten years in hard work for the Lutheran cause in the Middle Colonies. Mühlenberg adopted America without qualification and in making his home in an English colony, he devoted himself to the spread of the English language. On his first arrival, although his own command of English was meagre, he started to teach some young men the language by reading to them from the English New Testament; and in education generally he was careful to give them a thorough training in English before sending them to Germany to finish their education.

In a country " where every servant can play the part of a schoolmaster, who makes his living by school-teaching in the winter and by farm-work in the summer", Mühlenberg wished to see a

system of public instruction inaugurated with adequate supervision, and even addressed the Proprietaries to this end and too retained came of the plan because of the expense. When the scheme for charity schools was proposed, Mühlenberg desired to co-operate with the Society in increasing the efficiency of the schools at New Providence and New Hanover, and in two petitions presented to the Trustees by Mühlenberg the recently built school-houses at New Providence and New Hanover were offered for the use of the German-English schools.

In order not to stir up religious animosities, the Trustees passed these resolutions:--

That the thanks of the trustees in the name of the honorable Society be returned to the Rev. Mr. Mühlenberg, and the several vestrymen and wardens for their kind endeavors to promote this useful undertaking by the offer of a school-house, and which offer would be accepted by the trustees, provided the German Calvinist congregations in the same township signify their approbation, and concur in the choice and situation of these school-houses; it being the resolution of the trustees, according to their instructions from the honorable Society, to manage the whole undertaking in such an equal and impartial manner as that no parents, of what denomination soever, shall have any reasonable objections against sending their children to any school that may be established for this charity.

In transmitting the resolutions to Mühlenberg, William Smith

wrote a letter advising that every effort be made to bring all in other denominations into agreement as to the use of the Lutheran school-houses. Mühlenberg held meetings for this purpose and as a result petitions were sent from New Hanover and Providence asking that the Lutheran school-houses be used, since only were they most conveniently located.

At the first meeting of the Trustees, there came a proposition from Mühlenberg that the Society procure a German press in order to advertise their schools. This was the more necessary since Christopher Sower had already begun to prejudice the people against the Reverent. Mühlenberg had himself attempted to start such a press but his other duties and his limited means prevented. He signified his willingness to manage it, however, if the Trustees thought it desirable to establish it. The proposal met with general approval and Benjamin Franklin stepped forward with an offer of a press which he had attempted to start without success. He would sell the press for £25 less than the valuation of any two impartial judges. Mr. Allen contributed £25 in addition and the press was purchased at a net cost of £159 6s. Pennsylvania currency. Anthony Armbruster was secured as printer and schoolmaster at £20 per annum, with an additional allowance for his printing. Mühlenberg could not undertake the management of the press but he prevailed upon the Rev. J. F. Handschu, and his resident in Philadelphia to translate, read proof, and exercise general supervision of it. (Mann: Life of Mühlenberg, p. 335).

A German paper was started entitled, "Philadelphische Zeitung von allerhand Auswärtiger und einheimischer Merkwürdiger Sachen. Philad. Gedrukt und zu haben bey Ben. Franklin, General Post-iter, und A Armbruster, in der Markt Strasse, das jahr fur 2 schillinge." The paper had moderate success and soon secured four hundred subscribers. Besides the newspaper, school books, Almanacs, and religious tracts including 10 copies of "The Life of God in the Soul of Man," were printed. (The last work printed by the Charity School press was a German book on Rules and Articles of War. Seidensticker: First Century of German Printing, pp. 47 and 48).

In order to preserve the religious teaching in the schools, catechists were appointed from different denominations. Mühlenberg was one of these being engaged for the schools of New Providence, New Hanover, Vincent, Chester County, and for Reading. The salary of the catechists is not definitely known but Mühlenberg signed a receipt for £15, July 24, 1755, for his services as Catechist "commencing from May 1st, 1755".

Because of the promptness of Mr. Mühlenberg in his use upon the opportunities afforded by the Society for the Propagation of Christian Knowledge among the Germans of Pennsylvania, the first school was opened in the house which the Lutherans leased at New Providence. February 18, 1755, the Rev. Mr. Schlatter installed the teacher, Charles Cornelius Rabsteen, of whom Mühlenberg said in his recommendation, he is a "true-born Englishman, a Pres-

byterian ored and besides his native English speaks indifferent good French and Dutch. He is much beloved by the people of all persuasion, for his decent and Christian behavior". The course of study which was provided embraced reading, writing and arithmetic in German and in English, together with the general truths of Christianity, and in addition the girls were to be taught sewing. The master was allowed by the Society £25 per annum with an additional £10 to his wife.

The school at New Providence did not thrive. At the beginning there were but eighteen children and as early as October of the same year a parochial schoolmaster was employed, indicating that the charity school had either ceased entirely or was of small attendance, limited only to the poor people of the vicinity. And yet, in William Smith's report to Mr. Chandler, for the year ending 1759, it is stated that fifty boys were in attendance at New Providence, although in the financial report of the same year there is no mention of any payment to the New Providence schoolmaster. (Harbaugh: Life of Schlatter, pp. 243, 306).

The school established at New Hanover, however, was more successful and continued in operation until July 8, 1789, when Muhlenberg was instructed to announce the abandonment of the German-English school scheme.

In the beginning, the New Hanover school affairs were in anything but an harmonious condition. An attempt was made to have a union school and trouble arose between the Lutherans and the Re-

formed and between Schlatter and his people; but Mühlenberg tells
the story in his report to William Smith:--"We had a public meeting with the Calvinist ministers and the elders and agreed,' who sorely as it seemed... Soon after our joining and agreeing, the
Rev. Mr. Schlatter came up to Fewhanover and delivered a sermon
relating to the charitable scheme. His people began to whisper
and murmur, and part of them saying; they would have nothing to do
with the free school, if Mr. Schlatter had a hand in it. Nevertheless both parties were ordered to send down (to Philadelphia)
their recommended school masters to be qualified in English. Michael Walter was sent down by the consent of the Lutheran congregation... but the Calvinist school-master had no liberty nor
mind to go down and learn English but remained at home and profitted by Mr. Walter's being absent. Your Reverency was pleased to
send hereafter an order to Henry Antes Esq. (Henry Antes was much
 interested in the education of the Germans and the accusations
 against them greatly disturbed him. From 1745 to 1750 he had a
 school of the Moravians in his own house in Frederick township.
 Fotterer: Perkiomen Region, p. 92). intimating that he should
have a meeting with the appointed Deputy Trustees to see whether
the two schoolhouses could be kept clean, whether or a new one
one could be built. The Reformed found fault with some of the appointed Deputies and some of them refused to administer. I called
the Lutheran congregation together and asked whether they would
stand to their former promise to bequeath two acres of the church

land. They affirmed not only, but promised to make a subscription and to give their mites towards a common school house, according to the charitable scheme and plan, but the Calvinists refused to subscribe the least towards a common school house, alleging that they had built their own. In the meantime the brief history of the Charitable scheme was done and sent up by the Rev. Mr. Schlatter. The Calvinists read the said History in their church publicly and some of the elders declared openly, that they would not meddle with the free school, because Mr. Schlatter would be Supervisor. I spoke to Mr. Antes and desired him to do his best for exhorting and bringing the Calvinists into a peaceable frame. He conferred with the Rev. Mr. Leydich and sent me word, that the Lutheran congregation might choose two men for Deputy Trustees, since the Calvinist congregation had by an order of the Rev. Mr. Schlatter chosen two Deputies already. It being done accordingly, Mr. Antes ordered the four chosen Deputies together with the ministers to meet at his house, on the 10th day of February.. . .

February the 17th, the two Deputies of the Calvinists came to Mr. Antes and told him plainly before evidences, that the Calvinists would have no part in the Free School, before they had sent letters to the Rev. Synods of Holland and enquired whether they thought it advisable to meddle with this common scheme and plan; and moreover they would send letters to England and enquire what men or person had represented the Germans so ignorant, black and rebellious? And since they have seen Mr. Saur's observations in

his Newspapers and the scandal A. ? Clane Mr. Saur has imposed upon the innocent charitable scheme and the Rev. Mr. Schlatter, they are glad that their eyes are opened and have not meddled with the scheme and state he too, that I had a mind to ensnare them. The elders of the Lutheran congregation and their chosen Deputies are easy and have nothing to say against the Rev. M. Schlatter, Supervisor, and wait, what the honorable Trustees General will please to determine in this matter. (Mühlenberg to Smith, March 6, 1755.

In the "Weekly Messenger of the Reformed Church", Nov. 8, 1849).

Mühlenberg asks, "Should a parcel of whimsical heads have so much influence as to deprive a number of poor children of the charity?" To which the Trustees-General answered, "No" and a school was started under Mr. Walter, who was also the last schoolmaster engaged to whom Muhlenberg paid £18 at the closing of the school, his salary for three-quarters of a year.

The influence of Sower was already being felt and so great was the uproar created, that in the Coetus of the Reformed Church held at Lancaster, April, 1755, it was resolved, if possible, to frustrate Sower's mischievous influence. This opposition and prejudice of Sower to Schlatter and the churches under his care, ultimately caused his withdrawal from the supervision and in a measure accounts for the little success of the schools even with the Reformed, among whom and in a sense, under whose auspices, the undertaking was started.

In his capacity as Visitor, the Rev. Michael Schlatter was

subject to the orders of the Trustees in Philadelphia and it was because of his connection with the Rev. William Smith that he fell into disrepute since the base insinuations which Smith threw out were ascribed to Schlatter. When the Germans read these expressions of opinion and supposed them to come from their frequent visitor, Michael Schlatter, it is not to be wondered at that their blood boiled. In 1757 the feeling against Schlatter had grown to such dimensions that he was compelled to withdraw from apparent connection with the scheme and the whole management of the schools fell upon Mr. Smith. The magnitude of the work may be seen in the following instructions which, at the outset, the Trustees sent to Mr. Schlatter:--

       Philadelphia, February 12th, 1755.

 Rev. Sir: As you are appointed visitor of the intended schools to be opened by us for the benefit of the poor Protestant Germans, you will please observe the following directions in the journey you are now about to begin through the several counties of this Province:

 1st. According to the terms of the printed case, you will please converse with the People on the spot, and assist them with your advice in any designs they may project in order to obtain the Society's Bounty for encouraging schoolmasters among them.

 2d. You may receive the proposals and petitions of persons deserving the benefit of a school in the terms of the printed case; assist and direct the people in choosing the fittest places to fix

the school is; and with your advice and that of the several ministers, let them recommend Catechists and Deputy Trustees in their
Petition. The Calvinists two or three for each school, and the
Lutherans an equal number, unless perhaps there be any places
where the latter are not so numerous.

3d. If any of your own Clergy are straitened by the smallness
of their livings, and have anything to propose concerning the aug-
mentation of them, you are desired to bring their proposals to us;
and if you can recommend them as pious, industrious men, and
friends to the benevolent designs of the generous society, they
will be immediately relieved and assisted according to the terms
of the printed case. We rely on your own Judgment as to every material transaction, that when you return you may lay the proper
information before us, to enable us to answer the expectation of
those who repose so important a trust in us (any proposals made
for a school to instruct your ministers will be encouraged). You
are desired to acquaint Mr. Richard Jacob and the eight other gentlemen who favored us with a letter concerning the schools at New
Providence, That as we have not yet opened that school in the society's name, we leave it to Mr. Mühlenberg, Mr. Leidig, and them,
with your advice, to fix the numbers to be admitted into the
schools. We cannot open it until the month of April, but we shall
give the master a sufficient Gratuity for any poor children he
teaches, and the subscribers to the school shall not be desired to
pay anything more than they shall think reasonable. The Master at

present should not take more than he can manage, and afterwards we
shall settle all these matters by Rules, either when the schools
grow numerous to get new masters in them, or open new schools as
far as the society's fund will extend. We pray God to direct and
strengthen you in your fatiguing journey, and are, Rev. Sir,

    Yours, etc.,

      James Hamilton,

      William Aller,

      Richard Peters,

      William Smith.

To Rev. Mr. Schlatter.

  The town of Easton, in 1755, was one of those frontier places, settled principally by the Germans, at which it was proposed to locate a charity school. At this time scarcely a hundred persons, men, women, and children, had settled there. Three years previously, when Easton became the county seat of the newly formed Northampton county, only seven families wintered at the place entrance to the town being by means of an Indian trail. (Davis: Bucks County, p. 592). The chief citizen of this German hamlet was an Englishman, William Parsons, formerly the Surveyor General of the Province. Parsons had been a member of Franklin's club in Philadelphia and, on his removal to Easton, he was made the first prothonotary of the county. He was deeply interested in the education of the settlers and, with others, made application to Provost William Smith for financial aid from the Society. The surarntee

was 230. To this William Parsons and other citizens and friends added their contributions making a total of £81 1s, besides donations of labor and building material. A large, three-room schoolhouse which at times might be used as a place of worship was erected in 1755. One of the rooms was an assembly-room and the other two were smaller for the accomodation of the schoolmaster and his family. (Rupp: History of Northampton, Lehigh, Monroe, Carbon, and Schuylkill Counties, p. 395).

All denominations, including the Catholics, joined in erecting the schoolhouse which was located at the northeast corner of Sitgreaves street and Church alley. On July 21, 1755, the subscribers to the schoolhouse entered into the following agreement:

"We, the subscribers, being truly sensible of the great advantages our posterity may reap from the excellent charitable scheme lately formed in England, for the Education of Protestant youth in Pennsylvania, and being extremely desirous to encourage and promote the same as far as in our power lies, have engaged and agreed, and hereby do engage and agree, to and with William Parsons, James Martin, Peter Trexler, Esquire, John Lefebre, Lewis Gordon, and Peter Kichline, Deputy trustees, mentioned and appointed by the trustees-general of the said charitable scheme, that each of us will pay the sum of money, and do and perform the work, labor, and service, in building and erecting a school-house, which occasionally be made use of as a church for any Protestant minister, to our names hereunto respectively set down and affixed." (Rupp: His-

tory of Northampton, Lehigh, Monroe, Carbon, and Schuylkill Counties, p. 395-397).

We add a list of the donors to the school building as furnishing an excellent concrete instance of the interest taken by the people in education. It is note-worthy that the list contains the names of more heads of families than at that time resided at Easton.

	£	10s	00d
William Smith, in behalf of the proprietor and trustees	230		
William Parsons	5		
Lewis Gordon	3		
Nicholas Scull	3		
Nathaniel Vernon	3		
Peter Kichline	2		
Christian Rinker	1		
Jacob Eschman	1		
Jacob Winor	1		
Jacob Yohe	1		
Lewis Knauss		10	
Lewis Klotz		10	
Henry Becker		7	6
George Michael Shortz		15	
John Sevitz		15	
Anthony Esor		15	
Charles Reichart		15	

John Wagle   12   0 s   00d
George Ernest Becker   1
John Rinker   10
J. N.   7   6
Daniel Beese   5
Jeremiah Candy Russel   1
Paul Miller   1   5
John Ficker   1   6
                                       -------   ---------
               Pennsylvania currency   £61   1s

Myer Hart, 20 pounds nails
Paul Feesor, 1000 shingles
Jacob Wirer, 12 days' work
Stephen Horn, 1 week's work
Henry Allshouse, 5 days' work
John Horn, 5 days' work
John Finley, 6 days' work
John Nicholas Reeder, 1 week's work
Bartholorew Hoffman, 5 days' mason's work
Robert Miller, 4 days' mason work
John George Bush, 5 days' carpenter work
Jacob Kretz, 5 days' carpenter work
James Fuller, 5 days' stone digging
John Chapman, 3 days' carting stone
Henry Finker, 30 bushels lime

Henry Bush and John Wideman, 30 wagons stone and digging
Thomas Harris, 50 sash lights..

(Rupp: History of Northampton, Lehigh. Monroe, Carbon, and Schuylkill Counties, pp. 395-397). This list is quoted by Rupp from an account of this school published at Easton sometime before 1845 (the date of Rupp's book) by a Mr. Hetrick, probably in his paper, "The Whig and Journal". I have been unable to verify this. Superintendent William W. Cottingham of Easton, in a letter to the writer, states that in preparing his report of 1877 he had this document in his possession. (See also, Report of the Superintendent of Public Instruction, Pennsylvania, 1877, p. 692).

May 16, 1755, the Easton school was opened with John Middleton as master at a salary of £30 a year. (Smith: Life of William Smith, i, p. 92). Easton was a favorite place for holding treaties with the Indians and, on the outbreak of the war, it suffered greatly from Indian attacks. Accordingly this school, as well as the one at Codorus, in York county, did not continue long in operation.

Although the Society for the Propagation of Christian Knowledge among the Germans of Pennsylvania projected the establishment of schools for girls, the Trustees-General of Philadelphia were not quite so clear as to their necessity. In his report to Secretary Chandler, April, 1755, William Smith states that there is no pressing need for a large number of gilrs' schools at first.

(Perry: Historical Collections, ii, #51). William Parsons early saw that the neglect of the girls was a serious defect in the plan and, under date of October 19, 1754, thus writes to Rev. Richard Peters, Secretary of the Provincial Land Office: "One thing I think has not been sufficiently attended to---. . . As mothers have the principle direction in bringing up their children, it will be of little use that the father can talk English if the mother can speak nothing but Dutch to them; in this case the children will speak their mother-tongue. It therefore seems to me quite necessary that there should be English schoolmistresses as well as schoolmasters and the girls should be taught something of the use of the needle as well as to read and write (if writing should be thought necessary for girls). By the use of their needles the mistresses will have an opportunity of teaching them and making them fond of English dress, which will have great influence on their minds all their lives after, and if the young women affect the English manner in their dress and speaking, I need not mention how industrious young men will be generally to appear in their habit, and to speak the language which they think the most agreeable to the female world. It is the same in this respect in regard to low as well as to high life. Nature is the same in every station, and we differ only as we are educated." Doubtless as a result of this plea, in the school which was started at New Providence, February 16, 1755, the wife of the master was granted £10 per annum for teaching reading and sewing to eighteen poor

children, and later, a number of schools for girls were started.
(Smith: Life of William Smith, i, pp. 86,88).

These are not the arguments which would now be advanced for the education of girls. They reflect not only the chief purpose of the schools, the Anglicization of the Germans, but also the one-sided pedagogical notions of the time. Girls are not to be educated because education is the right of every individual, but because their use of the English language would instil it into the rising generation. The phrase, "if writing should be thought necessary for girls," is significant.

Although the contributions were intended solely for the benefit of the Germans, the Presbyterians made application for aid from the fund. They had established a school for the training of ministers, ten years before, but found that it was a very great tax upon their congregations. Accordingly, May, 1755, it was "ordered that application be made to the Trustees of the German schools to procure a sum of money to encourage our schools, engaging to teach some Dutch children the English tongue, and three or four boys Latin or Greek, as they offer themselves. . .If the sum obtained be less than twenty pounds currency, and not less than fifteen pounds, the Synod shall allow the school five pounds."

(Records of the Presbyterian Church in the United States, p. 219) After considerable discussion, the Trustees decided to grant £20 sterling. It does not appear whether this contribution was made annually but in 1762 Dr. Allison acknowledged the receipt of a

contribution for the school but stated to the Presbyterian Synod that it was very unlikely that they would receive any more. (Harbaugh: Life of Schlatter, p. 309).

The available records of the schools that were started are very meagre, and in most cases we have merely the name of the location. Eleven schools thus appear, seven of which were opened before July 1, 1755. These were :- New Providence, Upper Salford, Reading, Tulpehocken and Heidelberg Township, Vincent Township, Easton, and Lancaster. Other schools were New Hanover, York, Codorus, in York county, and Pikestown.

It was found rather difficult to find properly equipped teachers for these schools who at the same time would be acceptable to all parties. At Upper Salford, the Rev. Frederick Schultz was engaged as teacher. He was a roving missionary who had been educated at Halle and was for some a teacher in Francke's Orphan-House. He was of rather erratic temperament and seems to have divided his time pretty equally between preaching, teaching, practicing medicine, farming, and in a search for the "elixir of life", the "philosopher's stone", etc. For Tulpehocken and Heidelberg, Mr. John Davis from Ireland was engaged. For Vincent Township no available candidate appeared, but Mr. John Louis Ache was selected with the proviso that he attend the Academy at Philadelphia, at the expense of the Proprietaries, until he had become better acquainted with the English language. Lancaster was more fortunate in the employment of the Rev. Samuel Magaw.

It was at Lancaster, a town of about five hundred houses, that the Trustees established a school of higher grade. At the time the scheme was started the Germans in Lancaster had good schools under the care of both the Lutheran and the Reformed Churches but there were no opportunities for higher education. Accordingly the ministers of the two chief churches joined with fourteen other prominent men of the town in asking aid for a school where Greek and Latin might be taught:--

To the Trustees-General of the Charitable Scheme for the instruction of Poor Germans in the Province of Pennsylvania:

The Petition of divers of the inhabitants of the Borough of Lancaster in behalf of themselves, and others of the German nation residing in the said Borough, and parts adjacent, humbly sheweth that the number of poor Germans in these parts is very considerable, as well as those who are of ability to pay for the education of their children, if proper schools for that purpose wer^e opened, and your Petitioners, having a just and lively sense, not only of the many Benefits attending a competent Knowledge of the English language in their commerce and intercourse with divers unacquainted with the German tongue, out also of the pleasures resulting from anUnity of Languages, greatly conducive to an unity of sentiments, do Humbly pray that they may partake of the bounties of the charitable Society in London; that a school may be opened in this Borough by the Trustees-general for teaching the English language in Pursuance of the said Charitable Scheme, and that the said

Trustees would be pleased to appoint and send a sober, discreet and religious Gentlemen, capable of fulfilling this trust and answering the benevolent intentions of said Society. As divers of the inhabitants of this Borough are desirous of having their Children instructed in the Latin and Greek Languages, but from the smallness of their numbers are unable to support a master for that purpose, your petitioners request that a gentleman acquainted with these learned languages may be appointed, that the desires of these inhabitants may be gratified, but in a way not prejudicial to the principal design.

As there are two German schools—one of the Lutheran, and the other of the Calvinists Congregations—already in this town; and the Germans are unable to educate their own poor children in the German languages together, as it would occasion confusion; your petitioners pray that the charity designed for this purpose may be given to the masters of the respective Congregations.

Posterity, whose welfare and happiness will be chiefly increased by this charitable Institution, will doubtless be filled with the warmest sense of gratitude to the authors of this Benefaction, and as your petitioners are unanimous in their wishes for the success of it, their utmost efforts will not be wanting in the promoting of it.

Lancaster, December 28th, 1754.

Recognising that such a school was scarcely of a character in accord with the plans of the Trustees, several men contributed an

aggregate sum of £54 for the expenses of the first year. The teacher selected was Samuel Magaw who was then in the Philadelphia Academy and boarding with the Rev. Peter Brunnholtz, a Lutheran minister, who was acting as his guardian. Mr. Magaw was required to make more progress in the German language before he was permitted to take charge of the school. Mr. Magaw afterwards became a Doctor of Divinity, Rector of St. Paul's Church, Philadelphia, and Vice-Provost of the University of Pennsylvania. The school was opened July 1, 1755, and the Trustees granted an allowance of £25 to aid in the employment of an usher.

The chief attention of the Trustees was devoted to the establishment of schools in the outlying towns. Such a place was Reading founded in 1748; Mr. Schlatter said in 1750 that there were sixty houses there and, in 1751, the population was only 378 which, 1769, had risen to about a thousand. (Day: Historical Collections, p. 133). Rev. Philip Jacob Michael stirred up the people of Reading to apply for aid and early in December, 1754, the Trustees received their petition for a school and resolved to start one as soon as possible: in March of the following year the school was in operation.

The salaries of the masters ranged between £20 and £30, Pennsylvania currency, per annum, equal to £53 to £80. In most of the schoolhouses there were accomodations for the master and his family and frequently there was a garden for his use. The total expense of the management of the schools in 1756 is stated to be

£400 per annum.

The course of instruction, with the exception of the school at Lancaster, was scarcely in advance of that of the church schools which they were to supplant. The only additional subjects were the English language and, possibly, sewing. In the church schools, singing and "the principles of Christianity" had long been taught and we are led to suspect, from the complaints that were made, that these subjects were not particularly well taught under the new regime.

Now what shall be said of the general success of these German-English schools. In the report of the Pennsylvania Trustees to the Society in London, September 24, 1756, it is stated that "upon the whole, they are in as promising a state as can reasonably be expected in a Country so much harassed by a savage Enemy, and subject to so many Alarms to disturb that Peace and Tranquility which are so essentially necessary to the Cultivation of Knowledge. You are already informed that three of theSchools We had planted have for some Time past been entirely broken up, being near the Frontiers, where the People have for near a year have been flying from Place to Place and but little fixt in their Habitations." (Smith to Chandler; Perry: Historical Collections, ii, pp. 58.-332).

In a letter from Dr. Chandler to the Rev. Mulenberg, an extract from Dr. Smith's report to the Society in London is preserved for the year 1760,--

"Schools were then kept at the following places,--

New Provicence, in Philadelphia county,	50	boys
Upper Dublin,	45	"
Northampton, in Bucks county,	60	"
Lancaster, in Lancaster county,	65	"
York, in York county,	66	"
New Hanover, in Berks county,	45	"
Reading, in Berks county,	32	"
Vincent, in Chester county,	45	"
Presbyterian School, where are educated for the Holy Ministry,	25	youngmen.

These numbers refer to the autumn of 1759 when harvesting was going on. In winter these schools frequently contained six hundred pupils; "and, before the invasions and butcheries of the Indians, when those of Easton and Cocorus were in a flourishing condition, the number rose as high as seven hundred and fifty." (Harbaugh: Life of Michael Schlatter, pp. 302,307). As the schools declined rapidly after this date, we may place the maximum attendance at seven hundred and fifty, certainly a small return for all the money, all the diplomacy, all the suspicions, all the bitter hatreds. But colonial Pennsylvania was not a bed of roses for philantropists, officials, or even political schemers.

The attitude of the Friends toward the scheme was, to say the least, that of passivity. The charge that has frequently been made that Sower was hired by the Friends to obstruct the schools is undoubtedly unjust and it is quite reasonable to expect that

Sower could guess at the political purposes of the schools and it would have been strange, indeed, if he as well as all other educated Germans had not been exasperated at the language Smith used in speaking of the Germans. The Friends bitterly hated Smith for his action in seeking to alienate the peace-loving sects and also for ~~for~~ his political ideas. Smith was an ardent adherent to the interests of the Proprietaries and a zealous worker for the Episcopal Church and in the period we are considering both these were opposed to the Friends. The feeling ran so high that when Smith caused to be published in the Society's paper a memorial in justification of Judge William Moore, he was thrown into prison and the usual rights of the accused were refused him by the Quaker Assembly. On Smith's appeal to the Crown, however, the Pennsylvania Assembly was rebuked for its unwarranted conduct---but this belongs to the politics of the time.

The Reformed Church early became disaffected. In 1755, the Rev. William Stoy wrote to the Fathers in Holland complaining than English rather than German was being taught and that there was very little religious instruction in the schools. Moreover, the men in charge were not particularly moral men and instead of charitable and philanthropic ends he scented political trickery. The Coetus again addressed the church dignitaries in 1757 saying: "It may be said, however, that we can do little towards advancing the schools because the directors are bent on making them all English, and care nothing for the German language. Hence, now as before, the

Germans ought themselves to look out for schools in which their children may be trained upon the German mode." Another strong objection from the standpoint of the Reformed Church was the fact that in such schools as had been established there were marked preferences given to Lutherans because of their closer relationship to the Anglican communion. Indeed, Mr. Smith even entertained thoughts of bringing the whole Lutheran Church into the Episcopalian fold. Writing to the Bishop of Oxford, he says, "Your Lordship may depend that they (the schools) shall always be conducted with a due regard to the Interest of the Church of England. For in truth it is but one part of the same noble Scheme in which the Ven.^{ble} Society (the Society for the Propagation of the Gospel) are engaged, & wherever there are Missionaries near any of the Schools, they are either employed as Masters, or named among the Deputy Trustees & Managers of the Schools. In short, until we can succeed in making our Germans speak English & become good Protestants, I doubt we shall never have a firm hold of them. (Perry: Historical Collections, ii, 500).

Chapter VI.

THE DECADENCE AND CLOSING OF THE SCHOOLS

AS A result of the Provisions of William Penn for absolute religious liberty in his colnoy, these Germans settled here. They came from a country in which they had been subjected to all kinds of civil and religious persecutions, and, in their simplicity, they expected to find here an asylum where they could live apart from the moral, religious, and intellectual currents which had disturbed the placid surface of their life in Germany. Instead, however, of becoming a people absolutely apart, they found themselves living under English institutions with which they were not in sympathy, and subjected to a ridicule which they could ill return. They found their legal cases tried in English courts the routine of which they did not comprehend, and they heard their sentences in a language they did not understand. This they submitted to as to the inevitable, and in doing so they considered that their civil liberty had been curtailed. Only religious liberty was left inviolate. Since the schools of the German people had been solidly parochial schools, they held fast to these schools as being a part of their religious organization. An attack upon their schools was an attack upon their religion, and as such was most strenuously resisted.

We must look to their religious beliefs for an explanation of

the general apathy of the colonial Pennsylvanians, English as well as German, to educational concerns. Since the very essence of their religious life was an inner experience, and since this inner light was absolutely independent of all intellectual ability, be it innate or acquired, schools other than those of the elements made no strong appeal to their needs. In a religion which is primarily dependent upon philosophical distinctions or upon logical form, a system of well developed schools is a necessity. Thus we see in the foundation of colonial education in Massachusetts, well developed schools coming early in her history because these schools were to train the ministers in a religion which made more account of the letter and less of the spirit. The same general tendency is manifest in the excellent schools of Scotland, where the people of influence in educational matters have been trained in a religion founded upon logical and philosophical distinctions. The Quakers and the pietistic German sects in colonial Pennsylvania needed schools which would teach simply the three R's, thus throwing open to the learners an avenue to all religious life, since it enabled them to read their Bibles. Meditation and reverie would add that inner experience which alone was worthy the name of religion. Along with such an exaltation of the individual, we would expect to see constituted church authority, forms and ceremonial, and, indeed, the power of the State over the individual gradually become less potent in their influence. On the other hand, we expect a high standard of personal morality, a living, practical

piety leading as a consequence to an abhorence of war and strife, and a steadfastness against the necroachments of institutional activity on personal initiative finding its expression chiefly in innumerable sects, separated by hazy and inconsequential boundaries.

The one man in whom all objections to the system of schools found most forcible expression was Christopher Sower. He was born in Wittgenstein in Westphalia, Germany, and came to this country in 1724, and settled in Germantown. Except for an interval of five years he lived the rest of his life in Germantown, engaged in those activities which earned for him an enviable reputation among the Germans. Says the "Acta Historico-Ecclesiastica", xv, p. 213, "He (Sower) is a very ingenious man. He is a Separatist who has become dexterous at at least 20 trades. For, having come over to America as a tailor, he has since become a printer, apothecary, surgeon, botanist, clock and watchmaker, cabinet maker, bookbinder, newspaper maker, manufacturer of his own tools, wire and lead drawer, paper maker, &c., &c."

Sower was a man of inflexible character. Certain things, certain influences he saw at work around him, he hated. In his early life he learned to abhor offensive or defensive war, and he could not compromise by making contributions for war purposes. During the Indian troubles in the middle of the eighteenth century, such a doctrine held by so many Pennsylvania sects was almost subversive to government.

Although Sower was a believer in non-resistance and would not even sanction an appeal to courst for the enforcement of his rights, yet he was most aggressive in his combat against organised church government. His ideal was the very simple organisation of the early Christian church. He hated regular ministers as being men specialized for preaching by a long course of study, whereas, in his mind, the single need of the preacher was a clear inner spiritual vision. He says slurringly of the ministers of the regularly establisned churches, "that either at Philadelphia or in New Jersey they would be forged and polished for their (the German's) benefit until they would be quite fit." This explains his decided coolness toward Mühlenberg, Brunnholtz, Handschuh, and Schlatter. As Sower was always unable to distinguish men from measures, his dislike of these intensified his antagonism to the schools in which they were interested.

It was as a newspaper man that Sower exerted his widest influence. His little paper (nine by thirteen inches), "The High-German Chronicler", was first issued August 20, 1739, as a quarterly; later it was changed to a monthly, and the title altered to "Pennsylvania Reporter". This change in title grew out of the fact that Sower had conscientious scruples against pretending that his paper was a chronicle, after finding that some of the matter he had published as news was simply rumor. Still later, in 1762, the son, Christopher Sower II., again amended the name of the paper in accordance with his notions of journalistic ethics, to the "Ger-

mantown Newspaper, or Collection of probable news in the realms of Church and Nature, as also remarks and instructions upon matters of general utility." This paper was read in almost every German household. In 1751 the circulation had reached the comparatively enormous issue of four thousand copies, and Sower had difficulty in printing his paper and distributing it. With such an instrument in his hand, he was an adversary worthy the steel of any opponent, and, as is shown in the sequel, his was the side that triumphed.

In reading the following quotations from Sower's writings, we must keep in mind his antagonism to an established church with salaried ministers, his notions of the emptiness of book-learning, his abomination of war, and, let it be added, his German carefulness in money matters. A graduate of Marburg University, yet seeing little value in secular education; a philanthropist giving money and service to the distressed of his own nation, yet being extremely suspicious of the Tax-Collector; a singularly upright man, yet sometimes stooping to unscrupulous means in throwing suspicion upon his opponents, Sower presents many contradictions of character which it is useless to explain away. They have their source in his intense feeling on all matters that concerned the German settlers and in the extraordinary energy with which he sought to improve their condition.

In the issue of his paper, June 26, 1754, he had the following: We hear that ambition, etc., has made a provision in the Academy

Of Philadelphia for Germans, who have no mind to get their living by honest labor, probably under pretext of raising lawyers, preachers and doctors, since so little honesty comes in from abroad. But as human weakness values things that come from far much more than what is daily in view; and, whereas, one has liberty in Pennsylvania to call a shilling a shilling, those that have got their learning from empirics shall expect but little encouragement in this country, since "a prophet has no honor in his own country."

(Smith: Life of William Smith, i, p. 48).

Again, September 1, 1754: In our number 159 we mentioned that a high school or college was to be erected at Philadelphia for the benefit of the Germans in the city of Philadelphia, Lancaster, York, Reading, Easton, etc., and that the Germans by degrees may become one nation with the English, and so make all of English ministers only. These accounts further tell us this was done out of fear the multitude of Germans might make up or form themselves into one separate people or body, and in time of war go over to the French, and join with them to the jurt and prejudice of the English nation.

The new Society in England deserves praise for being so liberal and so kind as to teach the Germans the English tongue gratis. But if Slatter has accused the Germans to such a degree, and represented them as if they were a nation of so roguish and mischievous a disposition; that in time of war they would probably join the French and villainously espouse their cause, he has most

certainly acted with great imprudency, to the disadvantage of the King, as well as of himself. None, indeed, will permit himself to think that many Germans could be so treacherous as he perhaps may think. The Irish, the Swedes and the Welsh keep their languages, yet for all that are not looked upon as a disloyal people. Oh, that truly pious schoolmasters in the English tongue might be given them, who could be to them a pattern of a true Christian life! Then still some n,,pes would be left, some good might proceed therefrom; for it is true piety only that makes men to be faithful towards God and their neighbor. The preacher Solomon says, chap. IX, v. 13, "Wisdom is better than weapons of war; but one single artful and wicked man destroyeth much good." The wicked man may preach English or German, yet it is to no purpose or benefit, for no soul shall be mended thereby, nay, not himself. (Translation by Mühlenberg quoted in Smith: Life of William Smith, i, pp. 68,69).

In a letter to Conrad Weiser in the possession of Prof. Martin G. Brumbaugh of the University of Pennsylvania, Sower sums up the popular objections to the Charity Schools.

       Germantown, September 8th, 1755.

Dear Friend: I received your letter, and answer it by the bearer. I have been thinking since you wrote to me whether it is really true that Gilbert Tennent, Schlatter, Peters, Hamilton, Allen, Turner, Schippin, Franklin, Muhlenberg, Brunnholz, Handschuh, &c., have the slightest care for a real conversion of the ignorant portion of the Germans in Pennsylvania, or whether the institution of

free schools is not rather the foundation to bring the country into servitude, so that each of them may look for and have his own private interest and advantage.

Concerning Hamilton, Peters, Allen, Turner, Schippin, and Franklin, I know that they care very little about religion, nor do they care for the cultivation of mind of the Germans, except that they should form the militia and defend their properties. Such people do not know what it is to have faith and confidence in God; but they are mortified that they cannot compel others to protect their goods.

Tennent may believe, if he pleases, that his religion is the best; and if it is possible that, with the assistance of Schlatter, English preachers may receive a salary in being called for the Germans; that such preachers should be educated in Philadelphia, or even if such ministers should be formed and polished in New Jersey, then has Tennent the honor, and Schlatter is provided for. But the Germans will no doubt elect for the Assembly, on account of their benefactions, Hamilton, Peters, Schippin, Allen, Turner, &c., &c.

These make a law, together with Robert Hunter Morris, for the building of a fortress for the militia, with a garrison; stipulate a salary for the ministers and schools, so that it will not be necessary to write a begging letter to Halle (in Germany) of which they are ashamed afterwards, and are considered as liars, when the reports are printed. Thus <u>the poor Germans</u> are the pretext, that

every one may succeed in his purposes.

I am here, as it were, hidden in a corner, where I hear the words and thoughts of many.

The one says: "I feel uneasy about having my children educated out of the funds of the poor, as I do not need it, being able to pay for it."

Another says: "Where so many children come together, there they learn more evil from others than what is good; I will therefore teach myself my children writing and reading, and I am sorry that so many children come to see my own ones."

Others again say: "If the German children learn to speak English and come in society with the English, then do they wish to be clothed after the English fashion, and there is much difficulty and trouble to remove from their minds these foolish notions."

I hear others say: "We, poor people, have no advantage from the benevolence of the king and the Society, if they do not build a school-house or keep a teacher at the distance of every ten miles. For, if a child is obliged to go to school and come from further than five miles, it is too far to do so every morning and evening; the children cannot be boarded, nor can we give them clothes to go to school with others of higher rank, and therefore this advantage is only for the rich and the English. Should people make petitions for their temporal and eternal ruin?"

I have a small English books on the principles of the Freemasons; my copy, printed in England, is the 3d edition. I find its

teachings very far from the kingdom of Jesus Christ. Indeed they are the very hindrance of it. The people, who are the promoters of the free school, are Grandmasters, Wardens among the Freemasons, and their pillars. I think they intend something else, from what they think to be their best.

* *

      Your friend,

        Chr. Sauer.

  Certain it is that the schools themselves but more particularly the manner of their establishment were an insult to the German people. No attempt was made by the Trustees to conceal their contempt for the Germans and in their occasional visitations to the schools they came with all the pomp and circumstance of the lord visiting his tenants. Not only were they very little in advance of the schools they supplanted, but the opening of such schools seemed to indicate that the Germans were unable properly to provide for the intellectual, moral, and religious education of their children. Add to this the very apparent political and religious bias of the authors and we are driven to agree with Christopher Sower, much as we may deprecate his methods of criticism.

  All these obstructionist proceedings were ultimately successful. Remembering the disturbed condition of affairs in Pennsylvania, with the Indians destroying frontier settlements, and the French and Indians combining their attacks; together with a Quaker Assembly weak in preparations for war and we have a very good rea-

son for the closing of the outlying schools. When peace was established, in 1763, England found herself exhausted after the seven years' struggle and her philanthropists not quite so willing to send money to America. Then, too, there was an increasing coolness arising between the colonies and the mother country. There was also considerable disunity among the Pennsylvania Trustees. Political conditions had changed and, in particular, Provost Smith and Benjamin Franklin found themselves enemies.

With the exception of the opposition of Christopher Sower, perhaps the chief reason for the closing of the schools was that their political raison d'être had ceased to exist. The power of the Friends in the Assembly had been broken. In 1764, Mr. Chandler writes to Richard Peters,--"As the (free) Schools, &c., in Pennsylvania are now at an End, tho' I could have obtained his Majesty's Bounty for the Continuance of them, had it been of any Consequence to have upheld them longer, you, Sir. and the rest of our worthy Trustees, have my most sincere and warm Thanks for the Care and Integrity you have shewn in this Affair; and I will take Care you shall have all due Acknowledgments of the Society upon their first Meeting. (Perry: Historical Collections, ii, P. 573).

As early as October, 1761, the Coetus of the Reformed Church reported that so far as they knew there were then only three of the schools in existence of which two were entirely English and one English-German school. The last of the schools was closed July 3, 1762.

Chapter VII.

CONCLUSION

IN THIS educational scheme of the Society for the Propagation of Christian Knowledge among the Germans in Pennsylvania, there is a slight suggestion of a public school system. It was the nearest approach to such a system of public instruction that Pennsylvania made before the inauguration of school reform under the free school law of 1834. This, like all other attempts at popular education in early Pennsylvania, was vitiated by the oft-repeated words "charity", "*gratis*" attaching to attendance at such schools a stigma which made them anything but the democratic institutions they ought to have been. The amended charter (1711) of the Penn Charter School strikes the key-note of so-called popular education in Pennsylvania, where in speaking of the advantages of education, it goes on to say, there is bred in the pupils "reading, writing, and learning of languages, and useful arts and sciences, suitable to their sex, age and *degree*, which cannot be affected in any manner, so well as by erecting public schools." Imagine a modern teacher of our public schools speaking of the degree of his pupils. The fact is that it was a long while before Pennsylvania learned to use the expressions "public education", "public school", in any other than the English sense. Their schools were public just as Eton and Rugby are public; anyone who can pay can attend them and

there are a few opportunities for the children of the poor to be educated *gratis*.

There were some points, however, in which this scheme was far in advance of the pedagogical notions of the time. Prominent among these was the importance attached to superintendence manifested in the employment of a salaried superintendent, or Visitor, as he was called, responsible for the administration of the system. Rev. Michael Schlatter was the first superintendent of the schools situated at Pennsylvania, at a salary of $175 a year. He served from April 20, 1754 until the middle of 1757 when on entering the army as chaplain, he gave over the supervision to William Smith, but even in the army, he maintained an advisory connection with the schools. (Harbaugh: Life of Schlatter, p. 310. Hinke: Parochial School at Reading.) Each school, besides being subject to the visits of the superintendent, was to receive stated visits from the deputy-trustees appointed for Lancaster, New Providence, and Skippack, Reading, Easton, New Hanover, and York; also from members of the board of Trustees-General at Philadelphia; "and now, what a glorious Sight will it be to behold the Proprietor, Governor, or other great men, in their summer Excursions into the country, entering the schools & performing their part of the visitation." (William Smith to the Society for the Propagation of the Gospel, Perry: Historical Collections, ii, 546.)

Besides the superintendency and the establishment of the central board of education at Philadelphia (for we may call this,

rather than the Society, the central board) and of tributary to boards having immediate charge of the schools, we see in Smith's letter to the Society for the Propagation of the Gospel, the importance in which he held the training of teachers and the hope he expressed that the Academy at Philadelphia might become a centre for the training of teachers for the schools of the province. The course he proposed to give candidates for teachers' positions is, judged by the qualifications of the majority of the teachers of the time, a very complete one, although modern normal graduates will notice the absence of history of education, psychology, pedagogics, and methods.

To every system of public education some objections may be raised. In the first place, it takes out of the hands of the parents the necessity for looking after the education of their children, and places a relatively unsympathetic person *in loco parentis*. This gives rise to many difficulties, not the least of which is the loss of all initiative on the part of the parents in educational affairs and the shifting of the responsibility of education from the parent to the state through the teacher. Then again, in a system of public education, religious, in contradistinction to moral, instruction is out of the question. Dr. Smith's plan, being a transition stage from the old church schools to the public school properly so-called, largely avoided both these objections. It is true schools were composed of heterogeneous material but they were small and the co-operation of the pastors of the neighboring churches made religious instruction possible. Thus there

would be avoided in the product that appearance of machine-made goods, that stunting of the growth of personality, that levelling-up or levelling-down to a standard grade, which is so notable a defect in most modern systems of public education. The distinctive characteristics of each nation and of each religious sect were to be left inviolate that each might make its peculiar contribution to the national character and well-being.

In one respect this school scheme was more liberal than the present system of public education in that at present the large body of people using the German language have no public instruction whatever except through the medium of English. It is granted that a system of public instruction may limit itself to the teaching of such branches only that are directly useful to the State and the individual may be disregarded yet it might easily be proven that education in both languages would appeal to more people in the German sections and by this means those sections where the public schools are not well patronized might be led to take a greater interest in education.

The whole charitable scheme was a strong acknowledgement of the power of education. The Germans had come to America simply at the request of Penn to settle his lands. They scarcely thought of owing allegiance to any government but when they speculated on their position they considered that they held fealty to an individual, they were in a sense the employees of the Penns. When England entered upon her struggle with France, it was only too evi-

dent that the loose union of the multitudes of Germans through their connection with Penn was too weak, there was no spirit of nationality, only a very weak allegiance to an individual. The charitable school scheme sought to nationalize the Germans, to bring them under the direct control of the English government and to put them in sympathy with it.

The great defect of this system, the defect which makes us necessitate to call it a system of public education, was that it lacked the element of local taxation, of local responsibility. The money for the support of the schools was to come from outside, the Society in London was little more than a finance committee, and the schools were, therefore, in reality charity schools. This objection which Christopher Sower urged against the schools was cogent and this one defect in the plan of education accounts for the limited support the system received from the very persons it was designed to help. Had the people come together in Town Meeting, as the people of the New England colonies did, and voted the money for the support of the schools, they would have entertained a respect for them and could not have been blind to the value of public education. But the German people had not been accustomed to self government and their educational institutions at home had been provided for them ready-made by the authorities, so that they had no choice in the administration of education. It is not strange then, that they had no adequate notion of its importance. As has been indicated there were other potent reasons for the decay

of the schools, but we have in the lack of local taxation an influence which, sooner or later, would damn any system of public instruction.

BIBLIOGRAPHY

THE material upon which this article is based is very scattered and the few titles in the bibliography is an index of the little that is known of the movement. As it stands, the list contains several titles in which the schools are scarcely more than mentioned but in which considerable side light is thrown on the topic in hand. It is to be understood, however, that the bibliography only covers Chapters IV, V, VI, and VII. With the exception of the writings of William Smith, Horace Wemyss Smith's "Life of William Smith" furnishes the most material. In writing the Life, he had some documents before him which, as yet, I have failed to unearth. "An Educational Struggle in Colonial Pennsylvania," by Prof. Martin G. Brumbaugh is a short and readable summary of the whole movement for and against the charity schools.

Benham, Daniel.—Memoirs of James Hutton Comprising the Annals of his Life and Connection with the United Brethren. London, 1856.

Brumbaugh, M. G.—An Educational Struggle in Colonial Pennsylvania Wickersham Press, 1898.

Church Records of the English Reformed Congregation at Amsterdam, vol. 3, 1701-1765. Manuscript at the Hague.

Dubbs, Joseph H.—History of the Reformed Church, German, American Church History Series. vol. 3.

Dubbs, Joseph H.--Historic Manual of the Reformed Church.

Dubbs, Joseph H.--Old Franklin College. Read before the Lancaster County Historical Society, February 4, 1898. Lancaster, 1899.

Good, James I.--The Early Fathers of the Reformed Church in the United States. Reading, 1897.

Good, James I.--History of the Reformed Church in the United States, 1725-1792. To appear in the summer of 1899.

Hallische Nachrichten.--Nachrichten von den vereinigten Deutschen Evangelisch-Lutherischen Gemeinen in Nord-America, absonderlich in Pensylvanien. Zwei Bänder. Erset Ausgabe, Halle, 1787. Neue Ausgabe, Allentown, 1886 und Philadelphia, 1895.

Harbaugh, H.--The Life of Michael Schlatter, Philadelphia, 1857.

Hildeburn, Charles R.--A Century of Printing. The Issues of the Press in Pennsylvania, 1685-1784. 2 vols. Philadelphia, 1885 and 1886.

Hinke, William J.--The History of the Reformed Church at Reading during the last Century. In the "Reformed Church Record," December 1898 and following numbers.

History of Northampton County. By various authors; published by Peter Fritts, Philadelphia and Reading, 1877.

Kretschmann, Ernest T.--The Old Trappe Church. A Memorial of the Sesqui-Centennial Services of the Augustus Evangelical Lutheran Church, Montgomery County, Pennsylvania. Phila., 1893.

McMinn, Edwin.--A German Hero of the Colonial Times of Pennsylva-

nia, or the Life and Times of Henry Antes.. Moorestown, N.J., 1886.

Mann, William J.--Life and Times of Henry Melonior Muhlenberg. 2d edition, Philadelphia, 1899.

A Memorial in the Case of the German Emigrants Settling in the British Colonies of Pennsylvania and the back part of Maryland, Virginia, etc, London, 1754.

Mittelberger, Gottlieb.--Reise nach Pennsylvanien im Jahr 1750 und Rückreise nach Teutschland im Jahr 1754. Stuttgart, 1756. Translated into English by Carl Theo. Eben, Philadelphia, 1898.

Perry, William Stevens.--Historical Collections relating to the American Colonial Church. 4 vols. Hartford, Conn., 1870-1878.

Records of the Presbyterian Church of the United States.

Rupp, I. Daniel.--History of Lancaster County. Lancaster, 1844.

Rupp, I. Daniel.--History of the Counties of Berks and Lebanon. Lancaster, 1844.

Rupp, I. Daniel.--History of Northampton, Lehigh, Monroe, Carbon, and Schuylkill Counties. Harrisburg, 1845.

Rupp, I. Daniel.--A Collection of upwards of 30,000 Names of Immigrants in Pennsylvania from 1727-1776; (with notes). 2d Edition, Philadelphia, 1876.

Rupp, I. Daniel.--Copies of documents in the "Weekly Messenger of the Reformed Church," November 8, 15, 1849.

Rush, Benjamin.--An Account of the Manners of the German Inhabitants of Pennsylvania written 1789 with notes by I. Daniel

Rupp. Philadelphia, 1875.

(Saur, Ch.).--Eine zu dieser Zeit höchst nöthige Warnung und Erinnerung an die freye Einwohner der Provintz Pensylvanien von Einem, den die Wohlfahrt des Landes angelegen und darauf bedacht ist. Germanton, 1755.

Seidensticker, Oswald.--The First Century of German Printing in America, 1728-1830. Philadelphia, 1893.

(Smith, William).--A Brief History of the Rise and Progress of the Charitable Scheme, Carrying on by a Society of Noblemen and Gentlemen in London, For the Relief and Instruction of poor Germans, and their Descendants, settled in Pennsylvania, and the Adjacent British Colonies in North-America. Philadelphia, 1755. This pamphlet of eighteen pages was reprinted in Franklin and Hall's paper, the Pennsylvania Gazette, February 25, 1755. Later, in Rupp's History of the Counties of Berks and Lebanon.

(Smith, William).--Eine Kurtze Nachricht von der Christlichen und Liebreichen Anstalt, welche zum Besten und zur Unterweisung der Armen Teutschen und ihrer Nachkommen in Pennsylvanien und anderen daran gräntzenden Englischen Provinzien in Nord-America errichtet worden ist. Herausgegeben auf Befehl derer zur Ausführung dieser Sache bestimmten Herrn General Trustees. 18 S. Philadelphia, Press of the Society, Anton Armbrüster, 1755. A translation of the preceding.

(Smith, William (?).--A Brief State of the Province of Pennsylva-

nia. London, 1735.

Smith, Horace Wemyss.--Life and Correspondence of the Rev. William Smith, D. D., 2 vols. Philadelphia, 1880.

Stoever, M. L.--A Memoir of the Life and Times of Henry Melchior Muhlenberg, Philadelphia, 1863.

Thomas, Isaiah.--The History of Printing in America, with a Biography of Printers, and an Account of Newspapers. 2 vols. Worcester, Mass, 1810.

Van Horne, David.--A History of the Reformed Church in Philadelphia. Philadelpnia, 1876.

Watson, John F. and Hazard, Willis P.--Annals of Philadelphia and Pennsylvania. 3 vols. Philadelphia, 1891.

Wickersham, James Pyle, Editor.--Report of the Superintendent of Public Instruction of Pennsylvania, 1877. Harrisburg, 1878.

Wickersham, James Pyle.--A History of Education in Pennsylvania. Lancaster, 1886.

www.ingramcontent.com/pod-product-compliance
Lightning Source LLC
Chambersburg PA
CBHW021836230426
43669CB00008B/983